The Girl Who Baptized Herself

The Girl Who Baptized Herself

How a Lost Scripture About a Saint Named Thecla Reveals the Power of Knowing Our Worth

MEGGAN WATTERSON

RANDOM HOUSE

NEW YORK

Random House
An imprint and division of Penguin Random House LLC
1745 Broadway, New York, NY 10019
randomhousebooks.com
penguinrandomhouse.com

LIBRARY OF CONGRESS CATALOGING-IN-PUBLICATION DATA
Names: Watterson, Meggan, author
Title: The girl who baptized herself / Meggan Watterson.
Description: New York: Random House, 2025. | Includes bibliographical references.
Identifiers: LCCN 2025008059 (print) | LCCN 2025008060 (ebook) |
ISBN 9780593595008 hardcover | ISBN 9780593595015 ebook
Subjects: LCSH: Thecla, Saint | Acts of Paul and Thecla | Christian women saint—
Biography | Women in Christianity—History—Early church, ca. 30-600 |
Feminist theology | LCGFT: Biographies
Classification: LCC BR1720.T33 W38 2025 (print) | LCC BR1720.T33 (ebook) |
DDC 229/.925—dc23/eng/20250430
LC record available at https://lccn.loc.gov/2025008059
LC ebook record available at https://lccn.loc.gov/2025008060

Printed in the United States of America on acid-free paper

randomhousebooks.com

1st Printing

First Edition

BOOK TEAM: Production editor: *Mark Birkey* • Managing editor: *Rebecca Berlant* •
Production manager: *Kevin Garcia* • Copy editor: *Ethan Campbell* •
Proofreaders: *Michael Fedison, Kimberly Monroe-Hill, Liz Carbonell*

The authorized representative in the EU for product safety
and compliance is Penguin Random House Ireland,
Morrison Chambers, 32 Nassau Street, Dublin D02 YH68,
Ireland. https://eu-contact.penguin.ie

DEDICATION

In *The Miracle* by John L'Heureux, a priest named LeBlanc gives a sermon about just how extraordinary Christ's love for Lazarus must have been—a love so fierce and unfaltering that Christ loved Lazarus back to life.

Then Father LeBlanc says, "On the last day we will be asked the only question that matters. Not were you good or bad. And certainly not were you successful, were you popular, were you rich. But this, only this: 'Whom have you loved back to life?'"

This book is dedicated to MANNA—Van Jones, Rahiel Tesfamariam, and Lilakoi Moon—for loving me like Christ loved Lazarus.

CONTENTS

Contents

Baptize

I've never been baptized. Not officially, anyway. And although I've had all the formal training to become a minister, I've never been ordained.

I have a Master of Theological Studies from Harvard Divinity School, where I trained as a feminist theologian. And I have a Master of Divinity from Union Theological Seminary at Columbia University, where I took that training as a feminist theologian and applied it to the New Testament.

Why divinity school and seminary?

I knew my voice about a forgotten, silenced figure in Christian history would be doubted. Because my voice as a woman is not the voice that has dominated and defined the field of theology for millennia. And also, I knew that I would doubt myself—not only my capacity to tell such a sacred story but also to feel worthy enough to tell it. This is why I studied where I did and for as long as I did. So that my voice might have the heft of academia and the courage of someone who believes in herself. And more importantly, someone who believes in the power and significance of bringing a voice of Christianity that was buried in the fourth century to you reading this. To you who might be changed from hearing it.

Feminism for me is the belief in the inherent rights and equality of all human beings. The word "theology" is derived from the Greek words *theos,* or "god," and *logos,* or "knowledge."[1] So, theology, put simply, is the knowledge of god—or the study of the nature of the divine. A feminist theologian looks critically at traditional texts and scriptures of the Christian canon to reveal the systems of power at work within religion as an institution.

And what I found during my training as a theologian was a clear understanding of why I've never felt baptism and ordination were meant for me. I found evidence to support my long-held belief that Christ's ministry was about challenging gender norms, not deifying them. And that it was radically, meaning at its root, about love. What I found was a form of Christianity that existed before the fourth century. A Christianity that was such a threat to the existing power structures within the Roman Empire that to profess your faith in Christ meant execution.

Why was it so dangerous to be a Christian before the fourth century? To start, as the brilliant author and activist James Baldwin explains, "Love has never been a popular movement."

This earliest form of Christianity was fundamentally centered on love, and this focus on love as an ultimate power decentralized the perceived powers within the Roman Empire.

This book begins and ends with baptism.

Baptism is an initiation, a ritual that symbolizes rebirth. Rituals hold energy. They are a chance to release the past, what used to be, so that we can start again. So that we can be present, now, in the life we have in this moment. Each action we take while performing a ritual actively draws a line in the sand between what was and what will now become possible. So that we can step from out of our former self and enter a new reality, a life of our own choosing.

There's baptism by fire, by water, by a constant stream of words that bless us from hearing them. Stripped down to its core, a baptism is a rite of passage. A threshold. It's a chance to recognize what has always been true, no matter who we are, no matter what we have done or said. Whether we ever go through a literal baptism or not, we have the choice to become someone new. It just might take several hundred egoic deaths to get there. But more on that soon.

Within the Christian context, baptism is a public testament of faith. It's a ritual act performed before a community of believers to witness and recognize a new member. And it's a profession of belief in Christ, as he is presented in the traditional Christian canon of the New Testament.

Depending on the denomination, it's a cleansing of "original sin," a concept that wasn't formally created until the early fifth century by Saint Augustine, who was the first to use the phrase—and who we'll have to get to know at some point. For now, though, let's just take in this fact, that the idea that what's "human" in us could be anything less than what's "holy," that we're born with some sort of debt we have to spend our lives paying back by diminishing our joy, by ignoring, sacrificing, and denying the body—this concept didn't arrive on the Christian theological scene until hundreds of years after Christ.

Whatever your exposure to Christianity, I want to suggest we attempt, as far as it's possible, to release, or suspend, or even just loosen our grasp of what it might mean to be baptized.

Because in this book, in this story I'm about to tell you, baptism is a form of resistance. It's a triumphant dissent, an act of disobedience, a ritual of rebellion. Baptism in this story is a public display of reclaiming a power that exists within.

INTRODUCTION

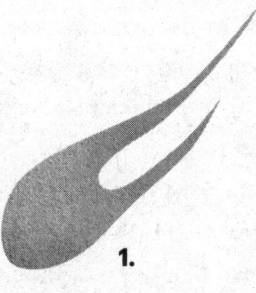

1.

Her Name

Let's start with this—a teenage girl is sitting at her bedroom window listening to a man share stories with a crowd next door. She's riveted by every word he says. And even though her mother and fiancé plead with her to stop listening, she refuses to move.

This man she's listening to is talking about a world that's entirely foreign to her, an inner world of freedom that will allow her to define her own life. And he's talking about love— not a love she has ever witnessed before. It's not a love that claims, but a love that liberates. It's not a love that asks anything of her, except to be true to who she actually is within her. And what's so radical about this world she hears him talking about is that it's open to everyone, including her.

There are no bars on the window she looks through, and her bedroom door is not locked. Her family has some material wealth, so she isn't suffering from a lack of practical things. But she's also far from free.

Her name is Thecla, and her story takes place in the mid-first century in an area of the Roman Empire that is present-day Turkey, where a girl like her would have little to no power according to the world around her. The man she is listening to outside her window will later become known as Paul the Apostle, one of the earliest followers of Christ. And the scripture where her story is found dates back to 70 C.E. and is titled *The Acts of Paul and Thecla*.

Her story, for me, reads like a lost gospel for finding our own source of power within—a power that allows us to know who we are and to make choices for our lives based on that knowing. Rather than perpetuating the relentless pursuit of trying to fulfill the expectations of others. And rather than letting the past dictate our choices in the present moment.

Thecla's story, and the scripture where it's found, suggests that women held positions of spiritual authority from the start. And it suggests that this earliest form of Christianity was about defying the patriarchal power structures that exist in the world, powers that seek to legitimate the idea that some of us are greater or less than others.

What becomes apparent when we take *The Acts of Paul and Thecla* seriously is that Christianity before the fourth century wasn't an institution, or even a religion; it was far closer to an ancient version of an equal rights movement.

So, what happened?

As a feminist theologian, I often feel like an archaeologist. I have to sift through the rubble of the erasure that Christianity underwent from the fourth century onward. I must read between the lines of the scripture within the New Testament for the scripture that I know is missing. I have to unearth what has always been there for us to find but that we've never been told existed.

I wasn't raised Christian; I was raised feminist. I inherited a sacred rage from my mother. And she inherited it from her grandmother. It's a rage at the refusal to be satisfied with a world that doesn't reflect the inherent worth of every human, or with language that doesn't actually name us.

I was taught to see and say the hard things, the unspoken things, to never fear a configuration of words that hasn't been said out loud before. I was taught that there's a rage love inspires that's the opposite of destructive. It's a creative force among those who have been silenced that feeds the resolve needed to trust in something unseen, unrealized in the world around us. It keeps us from accepting that this is just "the way things are." It's like an undiscovered fire inside us to insist on a world we can all imagine but haven't found the words yet to make visible.

So the cross signified more than faith to me. It also meant justifying slavery, genocide, the erasure of cultures; it meant generations of Native American children stolen from parents; it meant deifying the subjugation of people based on sex, race, caste, and gender. It meant controlling or taming women; it meant shaming sexuality; it meant Nathaniel Hawthorne's Hester Prynne and her scarlet letter. It meant condemning people for being anything other than heterosexual. It meant covering up abuses of power for men of the cloth, and excusing abuses of power for husbands over wives. It meant the Magdalene Laundries in Ireland, where girls had to do penance for being unwed mothers. It meant an adoration of an unattainable feminine ideal, and a desacralizing of the actual human reality—the sweaty, messy, bloody reality of the form of human body that reconstitutes the world, the form of body, ironically, that actually most closely mimics the divine power to give life. It meant unchecked authority; it meant immunity from any sort of real justice. It meant an absence of mercy when mercy was most needed.

The first time I read the New Testament as a little girl, I broke out in hives. I felt this intensely confusing mix of emotions. Before I understood what the word "feminist" meant, with little girl clarity, I was finely attuned to detect inequity. So when I went to church, and encountered this idea in the New Testament of a father god—and a father only—and that this male-god then gave some sort of holy decree for only male apostles and male bishops, and an exclusively male succession of divine authority going all the way back to Christ, I just sort of raised an eyebrow and quietly called bullshit inside me.

That inner sense, that inner knowing that there had to be more to this story, this is what led me to want to find the scripture I knew must exist somewhere.

And I knew this not because of any research or scholarship, not initially anyway. I knew this because of the love that liberates. And although there aren't words to adequately describe or name what I mean by that phrase, I will attempt to explain it in chapter four. For now, let me just say that this form of love I'm referring to wouldn't let me walk out of church, hive-covered and angry, and keep on walking. This love, which is more than an emotion or a feeling, is like a presence that came with me when I left.

French philosopher, mystic, and political activist Simone Weil described her spiritual position as located "at the intersection of Christianity and all that is not Christianity."[1] This is true for me as well, except for this one edit: I stand at the intersection of Christianity and all that is not yet Christianity again.

Religious scholars refer to the earliest Christian communities as "the early Jesus peoples" or "early Christ movements."[2] I refer to them collectively in this book as the Christ Movement. These ancient communities were so threatening to the Roman Empire that Christ was crucified for sedition, and everyone associated with him was persecuted. And for hundreds of years, up until Constantine claimed Christianity as the empire's religion in the fourth century, to call yourself a Christian meant being sentenced to death.

Why?

Women and girls, like Thecla, within the Roman Empire in the first century had little to no rights. Depending on their wealth and social status, women could accrue influence—secretly, behind the scenes, persuading their fathers or husbands—but they did not have direct power. Women only had access to a vicarious power. A proximal power. Because no matter their status within the Roman Empire, women could not vote or hold political office.

Thecla was not allowed to choose a life of her own. And this is critical context for us to understand before hearing her story. She was her father's property, then she would become her husband's. And her children would be theirs, her husband's and father's, not her own. It was a revolutionary act then for women within the Christ Movement to consider themselves equal to men, and equal to one another—to call each other sisters—even if one was enslaved and the other was married to a wealthy man with political power.

From the fourth century onward, the radical, highly persecuted Christ Movement that began in the first century was tamed and transformed under Emperor Constantine to look far more like the systems of power already in place within the Roman Empire. The systems of power that rank humanity according to a hierarchy of existence, with the emperor way at the tippy top, and women and slaves down at the bottom. In short, the Christ Movement became patriarchal. But it did not begin that way.

In 313 C.E., by a single edict, Emperor Constantine converted the Christ Movement to the empire's religion. By 324 C.E., he had assumed sole control over the empire and used the Chi-Rho, a symbol formed from the first two letters of the Greek word for Christ, on the shields and military standards of his warriors in battle.

Beginning with the Council of Nicaea, a council of Christian bishops convened by Constantine in 325 C.E., the church under the Roman Empire took all of the scripture that had so much to say about finding a source of power within us—a power greater even than the emperor—declared it "apocryphal" or "of doubtful authenticity," and then ordered for all evidence of it to be destroyed by the end of the fourth century.

Gratefully, rebellious monks, most likely Egyptian Christians known as Copts, refused to destroy the scriptures that had been deemed apocryphal, like *The Gospel of Mary, The Gospel of Thomas, The Gospel of Philip, The Thunder: Perfect Mind,* and *The Acts of Paul and Thecla*. Instead, these sacred mavericks buried the banished scriptures in caves and urns in the Egyptian desert.

When these scriptures were rediscovered, between 1895 and 1945 along the Nile, and in Nag Hammadi, Egypt, they were labeled "Gnostic," from the Greek *gnosis,* meaning "knowledge," because the common thread that connected them was their focus on the power we all have to *know* who we are—and that this source of power comes from within, not above or outside of us. The Gnostic label, however, relegated these ancient scriptures to something other than Christian.

In fact, all of these scriptures were and are foundational to the Christian story. They are not evidence of a separate religion or tradition outside of Christianity. They are evidence of its roots. These scriptures are evidence of a lost origin story about Christianity, a story about Christ that didn't win out.

When I piece back together the scripture that was deemed too doubtful to be included in the New Testament, Christ morphs from a blue-eyed, blond-haired, bearded man, holding a staff and telling women what they can and cannot do with their bodies, to a radical Middle Eastern man freeing women from the illusion that their worth could ever be dictated by someone outside of them. Christ morphs from a judgy, sex-shaming rule maker into a Jewish rule breaker who cared more about taking care of people than fulfilling the letter of an unjust law.

Thecla's story was lost to those of us who would have seen ourselves in her. Because after Thecla refuses to stop listening to Paul, she also refuses to be married off by her family. She refuses to be owned by anyone. She refuses to be controlled.

When the scripture that contains Thecla's story was excluded from the formation of what would become by the fifth century the formal Christian canon of the New Testament, what was lost was the power of what happens when a girl becomes her own. What was lost was the story of what happens when someone with no apparent power in the world around them claims a more ultimate power from within and becomes even what others deemed it impossible for them to be.

Why is Thecla's story important to us now, to you reading this?

Because we are all seeing out through a small window. This is what it means to be human. We all have invisible bars that keep us in our cages. And they all look profoundly different, these cages our egos feel most comfortable in. They're personal, individual. They're formed from the unbearable things that have happened to us. They are as varied as we are. It's the way out that's universal. And this is what Thecla demonstrates—the only way out is within.

Each chapter of this book begins with a passage from *The Acts of Paul and Thecla*. This is done with intention. It is done with the hope that in some not too distant future, Thecla will be famous. Thecla's story will be told around the dinner table, from the altar, in the grocery store aisle, at seminaries around the world, and on the playground in a huddle of little girls.

Her name, her story, her existence in the history of Christianity, her status as one of the earliest ministers in the Christ Movement, and her legacy of becoming her own, all this has been erased.

But here's the thing about erasure. All it takes is one person to remember. And for that one person to tell someone else. And for that someone else to tell a group. And for that group to tell everyone they know. And then, a lost scripture of the Christian story is found again. Not because it has finally been formally canonized. Not because it's officially deemed sacred at long last. But because we have remembered our own power to tell the truth. In her name.

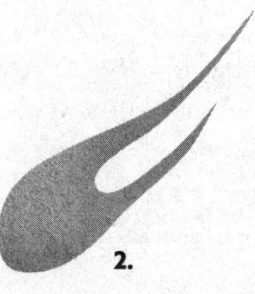

2.

Within

"Apocalypse" is derived from a Greek word that means to uncover, to disclose—to unveil the old and reveal the new. The apocalypse that most concerns me is the unearthing of these voices that were buried by the end of the fourth century. And to refuse to discount them—to take those banned scriptures, those silenced voices, as seriously as the voices that were canonized. As if all those words that were lost to us, relegated to the shadows, serve to correct our collective vision of what's sacred, as if we've been perceiving the divine like a cyclops, and now in our lifetime the other eye might open.

During the Women's March in the winter of 2017, which was the largest single-day protest in history, I heard the chants all around me, but I heard the echo of a more ancient one as well. It came from a passage in *The Acts of Paul and Thecla* that resounds within me whenever I need proof of what becomes possible when those with fewer rights or less political power are unified. It's this from a crowded arena at the end of Thecla's story: "And the women all cried out in a loud voice, as if from one mouth."

This one line from scripture, and its resonance in my life, made me return to *The Acts of Paul and Thecla* when the world stood still in 2020. Because it more than matched the intensity of the times; it read as though it was made for it.

When my son's middle school closed that spring, we established within the first week that I hindered his education if I tried to help. Especially with his math—which wasn't math at all. It was this "new math" that made me want to throw things. So, while my son "went to school" in the living room of our apartment in Cleveland, I burrowed into *The Acts of Paul and Thecla,* scouring its forty-five short chapters for the reason why I felt so compelled to study it again.

A certain popular quote began to pop up with an infuriating frequency back then. For years, I couldn't escape it in seemingly random TV shows, in conversations I heard, even once in a theater performance. It's this, often attributed to Albert Einstein and supposedly found in Narcotics Anonymous pamphlets from the eighties: "The definition of insanity is doing the same thing over and over and expecting different results."

Every time I saw that quote, it was gently, obnoxiously pointing me to a choice I kept making when it came to love. A love I just couldn't seem to let go of, or give up on, even though it kept ending in the exact same way. For over a decade, I was caught in a pattern. I would heal, or so I thought, move on, and start to feel free. Then, I would turn around, and without me realizing, there was my heart—in freakish perpetual bloom again in the center of myself for this person. My heart felt like a traumatizing Chia Pet. And I felt trapped. I wanted to figure out how to heal not only this relationship but also the strange addiction I seemed to have, the pattern beneath it, to a love that kept leaving me. In a world that is constantly making the same choices—repeating patterns that perpetuate human suffering—I wanted to find the power to mitigate my own suffering, to make choices in my one small life that would lead to what's next, to what's new, to what my perpetually blooming heart hadn't known before.

The answer for me came from Thecla's story—not just the content of it, but also the structure of the various stages of transformation she goes through. And it came from the single thing the entire world at that time was being asked to do: staying still. Staying still well beyond what's considered normal, or comfortable.

What's unique about the template in Thecla's story is that it's not the hero's journey—it is not the common mythological template, for example in the Homeric epic *The Odyssey,* where the boar-hunting and muscular Odysseus fights his way back to his literal and metaphoric home. This isn't the journey of someone who has power, who starts off already powerful. It's the journey of someone who has been told, and made to believe, that they are powerless and less than. This is the path for those of us who have been told we're unworthy to walk a divine one—and yet we still put one foot forward after the next. It's the template of transformation for a protagonist who has never been one before. Thecla's story models an ascension to power from within for those of us who feel powerless to make new choices, to start again.

Austrian poet Rainer Maria Rilke advised a younger poet, "Go into yourself and . . . examine the depths from which your life springs."[1] Storytelling—through reading or listening to a story being told—inherently draws us inward. The template of transformation that Thecla goes through in her story is not confined to the Christian tradition, especially since it unfolds centuries before Christianity officially formed as a religion. It's a process of transformation that's ultimately at the heart of what it means to be human; it's the path we have the chance to take anytime adversity comes careening into our lives.

There are seven stages to spiritual awakening in this story, and any good story is a story of someone who has undergone a life-altering change—a calling of some sort has arrived in their lives when they least expect it. That's the first stage: the jolt. Sometimes it's a crisis, a devastating moment of terror or loss. Sometimes it's far less apparent: the wake-up call. Sometimes it seems innocent enough, harmless even. Sometimes it just comes in the form of storytelling.

Some stories create a metamorphic shift in perception, a new way of seeing ourselves, our lives, the otherworldly worth of it, and what we'll do with the brief time we have here to live it. That's the second stage: a new way of seeing what might be possible for us. As if a door opens that we never even noticed was there. A now visible door opens, and from somewhere mysterious, from this newfound possibility we didn't even know existed, courage rises up in us to walk through it. This is the third stage.

Then there's the inevitable pilgrimage that this new way of seeing demands, compels us to take. And this pilgrimage, this adventure, inexorably forces us to unravel the old way of understanding ourselves and what's possible. This pilgrimage tests us to see if we're really ready to let go of how we used to operate in the world, of who we used to be. This is the fourth stage.

If we can survive the tests of the fourth stage, which tend to be both mental and physical and bring us to a point of choosing—of counting our losses and returning to what we had, to who we used to be, to how we used to live, even if we know how limited it is now, how small, even if we've tasted something more infinite—we're often given a chance to go back to what we know. To play it safe. To return to the traps and cages we once called home.

So we're often asked at some point to die. To go through a death that will mean a return is no longer possible, or at least that we can never return to what used to be, to who we used to be. We become someone new, which is terrifying. And if we can survive the death, if we can survive the terror of becoming someone unalterably new, we inherit power. Deep, true power. Power that only comes from within. This is the fifth stage. It's when all the perceived losses, and all the suffering, begin to transform into what the alchemists toiled away toward: gold.

That inner treasure has to be well-kept, held, and used wisely. This is the sixth stage. It's when we learn to own the hard-won power we've become. It's when we learn to take care of the self we have freed from the circumstances of our birth, from the world around us that wanted us to become someone else, the world that wanted us to be defined by what has already existed.

And what we learn in this sixth stage is how to be our own. We learn to be a self that has never existed before. We learn simply to be true only to what we hear within. Because we've completed this journey, because we've understood that all along, ultimately, no matter how far we traveled, the real journey took place from within.

And this is the seventh and final stage. It's the return to the place where the call first came from. It's a reintegration of that life before the revelation came. But it's an entirely new person who returns to the start. Or it's the person we already were from the beginning. It's just that now, we have become our own. We are no one else's expectations. We are no one else's possession. We are no longer the fulfillment of what others desire for us to be or become. We are now just the truth of who we are.

We have pulled back and reclaimed all the power we had been projecting onto the people and the places we called home. We have returned home, or we are now finally home for the first time, because all of that power is realized as something that had always been within us, sitting there silently, as if behind a small door, a hidden reliquary in the back of our back. The place we couldn't reach before because we didn't know it existed yet, because we didn't yet exist fully within ourselves.

THE FIRST STAGE

There are seven stages to spiritual awakening in this story, and any good story is a story of someone who has undergone a life-altering change—a calling of some sort has arrived in their lives when they least expect it. That's the first stage: the jolt. Sometimes it's a crisis, a devastating moment of terror or loss. Sometimes it's far less apparent: the wake-up call. Sometimes it seems innocent enough, harmless even. Sometimes it just comes in the form of storytelling.

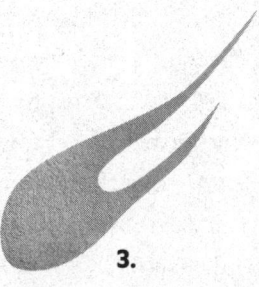

3.

Erasure

But Paul, gazing only at Christ's kindness, did no evil toward them but loved them so much that he made all the words of the Lord, the teachings and explanations of the good news, the birth and resurrection of the Beloved sweet for them.

—The Acts of Paul and Thecla 1:2

Hoigh on the northern slopes of the mid-Aegean coast of Turkey, there's a cave that has been considered a sacred Christian site since antiquity. It was discovered by a group of Lazarist priests in 1892, then rediscovered and excavated in 1906 by the Austrian Archaeological Institute. The restoration department uncovered frescoes beneath layers of plaster that date back to approximately 500 C.E. The cave was originally named for the Greek word meaning "hidden virgin," but was later renamed as the Cave of Saint Paul.

The central figure in the main fresco located near the entrance of the cave is almost entirely preserved. This figure is male, with a bald head, a beard, and the name "Paulos" etched in Greek letters just above him. His right hand is raised in a gesture, or mudra, of teaching-and-blessing according to Byzantine iconography. This is clearly, to most eyes, Paul the Apostle from the New Testament. However, this scene that he's depicted in is not a story that can be found in the New Testament.

To the left of Paul, a young woman is listening to him teach, not out in the open, but from her window in a redbrick house. Her name, "Thecla," is no longer visible above her head. Her name translates from the Greek as "the glory of god." She's right here, a significant figure in Saint Paul's life—significant enough to be included in a fresco with him—but without the scripture that tells her story, she remains unseen, unrecognizable.

Even if you're not Christian, or if you've only had limited exposure to Christianity, you've most likely heard of Paul. He's considered one of the most important figures in Christian history. Paul was previously named Saul of Tarsus and lived in the first century as a Pharisee. Pharisaic beliefs were the foundation of Rabbinic Judaism, which was founded in roughly 170 B.C.E. and dissolved around 70 C.E. According to the New Testament, Saul was among the powerful who were persecuting the disciples of Christ following Christ's crucifixion.

But on the road to Damascus, on his way to put yet more supporters of Christ in chains, suddenly a brilliant, otherworldly light flashed all around him. In the story from the ninth chapter of the Acts of the Apostles, Saul falls to the ground, humbled and blinded, and then he hears a voice ask him from within, "Saul, Saul, why are you persecuting me?"[1] Saul, understandably, panics, and quickly demands to know the name of the voice that has just brought him to his knees.

And the voice reveals that he is Christ, the one he's persecuting.

Saul remains blind for three days as he travels on to Damascus. Three is the symbolic number for death and resurrection. A disciple of Christ in Damascus, a healer named Ananias who had a vision that Saul would need him, restores his sight with "a laying on of hands." By chapter thirteen of the Acts of the Apostles, Saul of Tarsus begins to be referred to as Paul, to indicate the completion of his spiritual transformation.

I was familiar with Paul before seminary but less for his dramatic conversion story and more because he is somewhat notorious in feminist theological circles for declaring in 1 Timothy 2:11–13, "A woman must learn, listening in silence with all deference. I do not consent to them becoming teachers, or exercising authority over men; they ought not speak."[2]

Paul is also attributed with saying, as if in direct contradiction to 1 Timothy, in Galatians 3:27–28, "For all of you who were baptized into union with Christ clothed yourselves with Christ. There is neither Judean nor Greek, slave nor free, male and female; for in Christ Jesus you are all one."[3]

Read together, these two passages from the New Testament are antithetical, one condemning women to silence and submission, the other turning around and professing the radical equality of all humanity.

So what happened?

How do we reconcile the Paul who believes women should not become teachers or hold any positions of authority, in 1 Timothy, with the Paul who believes if we're baptized into union with Christ, we're then "clothed" in Christ and therefore we are all one, in Galatians 3:27?

The reason for this contradiction is almost as pervasive now as it was back then; it's about the power accrued by controlling women, our voices and our bodies.

There is a consensus among scholars that 1 Timothy was written well over a half century after Paul's death. So it was written in his name, but it was likely not written by him, nor does it necessarily capture the essence of his teachings. Perhaps it was written as a response, or as a form of an ancient smear campaign, a cover-up, to the Paul we find in *The Acts of Paul and Thecla*, who serves as a (somewhat reluctant) mentor to Thecla in her efforts to become a minister. Perhaps it was a way of bringing Paul to heel, of making sure he sounded more like a voice to reinforce the patriarchal dominance of the Christianity forming under Constantine in the fourth century rather than a voice to challenge it.

Unlike Paul, when it comes to Thecla, even if you're an exceptionally devout and well-read Christian, you have probably never heard of her.

What I want to make visible again, what I want to pull back from the erasure of Christian history, is the vision of a girl sitting at her window, listening to Paul's stories about Christ, and recognizing for the first time that there are no physical bars on the window in front of her. That her bedroom door is not locked, and that the most critical threshold she needs to cross isn't one that she can see outside of her. The most important threshold for her to cross, for any of us to cross, is so much more complicated and so much simpler than a window frame or a bedroom door. It's difficult, though, to remember and recognize something we've never been taught exists. Something we've actually been encouraged not to see. Something we've been blinded to even if it's right there before us in plain sight.

Paul's words, his "good news" about Christ, "the Beloved," changes everything for Thecla. Or it redirects and re-align the expectations she has of herself, of her life. This scene of a girl sitting at her window, listening to Paul; this is a road to Damascus moment that we've never heard before. Instead of fulfilling what others want her to be, as she's listening to Paul's stories, the stories he makes "sweet" for everyone listening, Thecla begins to turn inward. She begins to ignore the mandates the external world has placed on her solely because she is female. And instead, she listens to the dictates of her own heart.

Because she's a girl, she's expected to do what others want her to do. So this sudden freedom to listen inwardly to her heart, and to be so radical as to follow it, this is dangerous. Dangerous enough that Thecla will be sentenced to death twice, first at the demand of her own mother, and second by a man with considerable political power. The trials Thecla must face begin as soon as she answers the call. And for Thecla, answering the call begins by doing absolutely nothing. Or it's viewed, judged as doing "nothing" by those around her.

And maybe this is why the moment of listening inwardly is so significant in Thecla's story, this scene only half-remembered, only just barely still visible on the wall of the Cave of Saint Paul—because this is the moment when Thecla shuts out the exterior world and begins to answer that singular call that can only come from within simply by listening to it. An act that no one can control.

Maybe this is the most consequential part of Thecla's entire story, the moment her life changes its direction. From the expected to what hasn't been done before. From the external world to the internal world, the one that Paul refers to as a kingdom.

Without *The Acts of Paul and Thecla*, we are missing the

story of how the call to live a life mostly in relation to what we hear from within can come to anyone—even to those not invited, even to those just overhearing the words of Christ through a crack in their open window. Without *The Acts of Paul and Thecla,* we might be more easily convinced that only a certain circle of an elite few can hear the call.

We might be more easily convinced that it's too hard and complicated to put down the life that has been expected of us, the one most of us are living. And that the precise power needed to begin the life that was always ours to claim is too elusive, like chasing beads of mercury.

With Thecla restored from erasure, with the "hidden virgin" now visible again, we know that the nature of the call demands that it exclude no one. Because this call is a call to love, and it comes from within.

4.

A Love That Liberates

[Paul] described to them, word for word, the great things of
Christ and how they had been revealed to him.

—The Acts of Paul and Thecla 1:2

Love is not an emotion. It's not a sentiment, a fleeting feeling. Love is not transactional. It's not fair, or rational. Love is an actual presence. It's a presence that's within us. And it's more vast than I could ever name or that my own individual life can ever grasp. Love is an actual presence that calls us to be present to it, to be its witness if we can allow that small egoic self to quiet down enough to just listen.

Love is a presence that arrives often when we least expect it. And it asks everything of us. And what I mean by "everything" is that love does not figure the ego into its asking. Love does not care who our enemies are or what plans we've made. Or about what linear progress we want to make by a certain age.

Love is a presence that arrives and sometimes demands for us to be its presence, its hands and feet.

And it's because of love that I felt compelled to become a theologian. Because nothing enrages me more than a Christianity that sanctifies bigotry.

Love for me isn't something that I wait or long for; love is the beginning and the end of what I know of god. And for me, god is a love that liberates.

I can't name or point to one particular event, a "road to Damascus" moment when I first sensed or remembered it. "Remembering" is the closest word to describe it. The presence of love for me is like becoming aware of a memory of something I once knew completely, experienced directly, and yet somehow also then forgot about entirely.

So I am always surprised by it.

This love can't be described. But I'll try to anyway. Because I love the dare of a hard-to-reach place. I love to try to use words in the effort of reaching out beyond where words end. As if words might hold energy within them, as if each word is a tiny boat, so that even when this chapter ends, the words might still carry you somewhere.

The words might still carry you to the thing itself, out beyond them and the individual voice they contain, to the actual experience of what I am trying to describe. It's an innermost thing, a place that's often referred to as mystical, because what other word can be used? And "mystical" almost gets us there. But it's more. Plus, mystical is often misunderstood as something that's separate from us, separate from what's human. So, let's not call it mystical. Let's call it "the heart."

I felt this electric thrill the first time I came across D. H. Lawrence's description of "the very body's body," because I knew what he meant. Without entirely understanding it. It somehow made more sense to me. The body's body. It described to me something truer than just saying "the body." It felt like saying something deeper, something more profound. It felt like the direct experience of the body itself, not all that I impose or want or desire or expect of the body. It's just the body's body.

In the same way, the heart has a heart within it. And the heart's heart isn't human. Or it isn't human in the way we've come to understand what it means to be human. In the heart's heart, there's just unending, unmitigated, unspeakable light.

Unspeakable because no one can actually say where that light comes from—or they might say and claim to know this, but in truth, that light cannot and can never be fully named. This is what makes it sacred. And this is what makes us human—that we seek to know it and sometimes do, but then forget.

The light in the heart's heart is a love that liberates.

What most of us have known, what I have mostly known, is a love that claims. A love that possesses and seeks to own. A love that's terrified it will end. A love that tries to control. A love that wants to change what it loves. A love that has ardent roots in the ego. A love that is in fact not love at all. But we can call it love, because for most of us, it is all we have ever known.

And it's not that it isn't love; it isn't love yet. This is not meant as a judgment. I don't have the right to say anything critical about the ways we've tried and failed and tried again to love with our love that isn't really love at all. Because it's so tragic, and so gorgeous. And so brutally what it means to be here. To be human. To try with our egoic love again and again to love until we shatter enough so that we reach the thing itself.

We break enough or so completely that the veils, the layers, the masks come off, and we recognize that desire to control, that desire to have and to hold, that desire to possess, to claim, to always have by our side, that this isn't and will never be the thing itself.

The thing itself is here, with or without the ego. The thing itself is here in the heart's heart. And it doesn't claim. It doesn't own. It just radiates, like an open palm. Because it's not and has never been and will never be ours. It's a presence that's shared with us from within us. It's a presence that's shared with us because it's meant for us to then share.

It's a mandatory requirement for seminarians to be placed within a congregation that will allow us as mini budding ministers to practice all that we've learned. Since I didn't have a church that I could go preach in, a church that integrated scripture like *The Acts of Paul and Thecla* and *The Gospel of Mary,* and not just the scripture but also the theology of the early Christ Movement that these scriptures emerged from, I fulfilled my requirement instead in the neonatal intensive care unit (NICU) as a hospital chaplain at New York Presbyterian.

I floated between the incubators with their impossibly tiny inhabitants hooked up to a myriad of wires that created an oddly calming symphony of beeping sounds throughout the floor. I served as an all-purpose chaplain, since I wasn't actually affiliated with any church or denomination. I offered support only when asked. And I just tried to lend my presence to the space, a presence of inconspicuous love. Well, as inconspicuous as I could be in the tall red cowboy boots I was obsessed with wearing back then.

All day I just loved the impossibly tiny inhabitants of those tiny plastic huts, and I just loved the sleepless, stressed-out parents huddled around them as if their proximity could keep those reassuring rhythmic beeping sounds from suddenly changing into alarms.

And then the day came when I remembered the thing itself—right there on the over-sterilized, heavily Cloroxed floor of the NICU.

First, though, I have to describe the dreaded silence room.

There was a small sort of hermetically sealed-off room in the center of the NICU floor that everyone feared and avoided, from the nurses to the doctors and especially the parents. It was the only place on the floor where that pervasive cacophony of constant beeps and dings from the tiny humans in their clear huts could no longer be heard. When the door shut in the silence room, it was like entering another realm, or going underwater. Any parent who went in never came out the same.

As a chaplain, I was sometimes asked by a doctor or a nurse to accompany parents into the silence room. And most often, I just stood there, drowning in the thick viscosity of trauma. The blinding, sticky trauma of a newborn's death. I would just stand there and join the silence. I would rarely speak. Words didn't feel permitted past the threshold. Only silence matched the intensity of that dreaded room. Sometimes, I would put my hand in the center of a parent's back, when they were half their height, broken forward, and spilling their grief all over the floor.

But this one day, I was asked to do more. I was asked to join a grieving father standing in front of his tiny perfect unmoving daughter swaddled in a hospital blanket and placed in a clear plastic crib in the center of the silence room.

He looked up from the weight of staring at her, and looked over at me as if he were literally in that moment being physically crushed. He reached out his hand, and I took it, drawing me nearer to him, nearer to her.

Up until this moment, I had intentionally never learned the Lord's Prayer. The Lord's Prayer is the one that starts "Our Father, who art in heaven . . ." Most everyone, let alone a seminarian, can recite it. But I had made it nearly my mission to never utter or repeat it, to refuse to be a part of a tradition that sees and names god as a father and a father only. It was just too infuriatingly incomplete.

I couldn't even get past the first sentence of it without spiraling into a theological hurricane: "Our Father, who art in heaven, hallowed be thy name; thy kingdom come; thy will be done, on earth as it is in heaven."

The "Our Father" part . . .

This anthropomorphic idea that god is a paternal human male, a father, perpetuates a deeply engrained belief that males are not only entitled to inherent power due to their sex but also that this power is divinely ordained. An ideation of god as only a male, and not also female, and also beyond an expression of gender, places boys and men at the top of the hierarchy of existence. This has created and continues to create a hierarchical ranking of worth along a vertical axis. When in fact all of humanity is inherently worthy, and that worth is seen and known, along the horizontal axis. We are all theologically eye to eye, equally worthy of our existence.

The "who art in heaven" part . . .

The idea that there's this actual place, this "heaven," that is up, above, and beyond us, perpetuates a grave apathy and complacency about our impact on the natural world and the earth—this actual physical heaven we are standing on and are meant to be protecting. If heaven is an ultimate resting place, then the earth becomes in a sense an impermanent purgatory. Whereas if heaven is a state of mind—or heart, more accurately—that we can enter now through spiritual practice, while we're still living, as well as when we pass away into whatever might come next, then our sense of responsibility for the earth shifts and becomes more pressing.

Then finally, the "thy kingdom come" part . . .

This, again, perpetuates patriarchal dominance with the idea of a kingdom, which is a land ruled by a male leader—in this case, god. It's hard to even imagine the Christian tradition referring to "the queendom of god," or "the queendom of goddess." And this illuminates the inequity. The word "kingdom" is translated into English from the Greek word *vasileio* or *basileio,* which can also be translated as "royal power." This "kingdom of god," so often mentioned in Christianity, is more accurately referring to a royal power that exists within us. Not a human kingdom ruled by a man, but a sovereign power within every person. And this is just one example of a myriad of choices made by theologians in the past that have shaped the tradition of Christianity to comply with the same systems of power that Christ challenged. And this is just one example of why it matters that women were not a part of shaping the language of a religion that would ultimately suggest their voices have intrinsically less spiritual authority than men's.

For all these reasons, the words of the Lord's Prayer perpetuate a patriarchal version of Christianity that I've always sensed in my bones is not the whole story. So, I felt allergic to it. I felt physically incapable of saying it.

But then this father reached out for my hand, and in that heavy grief, his shattered heart became my own. We had a shared shattered heart. As he lifted his head, straining against the weight of her death, he said, "Pray over us. Please say the Lord's Prayer."

Instantly, I started racing through every corner of my mind for the words of the prayer I had intentionally never wanted to remember. What I personally believed didn't matter in that moment. All that mattered was what this grieving father had asked of me.

And so, I spoke each word only once—each word was finally remembered. It was probably the worst and slowest recitation of the Lord's Prayer he had ever heard, but every word contained the thing itself. Every word seemed to fill the entire room. And the dreaded silence was no longer silence. It was a stillness that let us feel how impossibly small we are, and how incomprehensibly vast love is. Love was the weight that bowed his head forward. He loved his daughter as if he had already spent a lifetime with her, as if he had already lived his entire life by her side. His love for her couldn't be calculated in the days and hours and minutes he spent next to her tiny incubator. That's how vast love is. It's out beyond time.

It's there in the silence, in the stillness, in that moment when a complete stranger reaches out for the hand of someone to pray with them. It's more than our religions and traditions and individual beliefs. It's more than any one of us can imagine.

And it's palpable. Love is so vast that it can fill up a dreaded room where death waits, fill the room so completely that the presence of that love is actually felt; it's physically perceived. As if love is standing there with us in those moments, when we eclipse our self to be there for someone else. When we let go of all our own personal ideas about god, and just be the presence of love where love is most needed.

5

The Word

And a man named Onesiphorus, hearing Paul had come to Iconium, went out with his children, Simmias and Zeno, and his
wife Lectra, to meet Paul so that he might welcome him. Titus
had described Paul's appearance to him for he had not seen
him in the flesh, but only in spirit.

—*The Acts of Paul and Thecla* 2:1

W hen I post on social media about scripture that
is not currently contained within the traditional
New Testament, I get a colorful array of not-so-
veiled death threats in the form of quotes from the New Testament (aka "the word of god"). For example, recently I posted
about Christ's explanation of the concept of sin in *The Gospel
of Mary* where Peter asks Christ, "What is the sin of the
world?"[1] And Christ replies, "There is no such thing as sin."[2]

Cue the incoming cellphone dings with each "word of god"
quote hurled into my account, like, "If anyone hinders one of
these little ones who trust in me, it would be best for him to
be sunk in the depths of the sea with a great millstone hung
around his neck,"[3] or "The devil, their deceiver, was hurled

into the lake of fire and sulfur, where the beast and the false prophet already were, and they will be tortured day and night forever and ever."[4]

What Christ goes on to explain to Peter and the other disciples in this passage from *The Gospel of Mary* is that we ourselves create sin, meaning sin does not exist inherently within us. We are not born or made sinful.

Hundreds of years after *The Gospel of Mary* was written, around the time it was deemed apocryphal in the mid-fourth century, Saint Augustine was born on November 13, 354 C.E., in Thagaste, northern Africa, which is modern-day Souk Ahras in Algeria. He is considered one of the most significant Christian theologians after Saint Paul. And similar to my knowledge of Paul before seminary, I had mostly heard of Augustine because of his raging misogyny.

Alongside the love-drenched and moving words of his most well-known work, *The Confessions,* Augustine also wrote, "What is the difference whether it is in a wife or a mother, it is still Eve the temptress that we must be aware of in any woman. I fail to see what use woman can be to man, if one excludes the function of bearing children."[5]

Biographies of Augustine reveal he had a son with a woman who then left him. Augustine's son died as a little boy, which precipitated his entry into the church as a junior clergyman in his thirties. He quickly became a priest and then a bishop by the end of the fourth century. Perhaps Augustine's personal pain fueled his perspective of women, which then shaped his interpretation of Eve. And as an educated man, born to parents with some means from an upper class of Roman society, his platform to promulgate his interpretation was far-reaching.

As Augustine was rising in the ranks within the church, he was influenced by a church father who came before him, a

man by the name of Tertullian who is known as "the Father
of Latin Theology." Tertullian is particularly relevant for us
because he was the loudest voice, in the late second century, in
labeling *The Acts of Paul and Thecla* as heretical. He resented
its overt implication that women can hold positions of spiritual
authority, lead communities in prayer, and baptize. Because
Tertullian believed that all women carried Eve's sin. He said,
addressing women directly, "You are the devil's gateway: you
are the unsealer of that forbidden tree: you are the first de-
serter of the divine law."[6]

Although Tertullian's criticism effectively diminished the
status and importance of *The Acts of Paul and Thecla,* enough
to make certain it was excluded, along with *The Gospel of Mary,*
in the formation of the New Testament generations later in
the fourth century, he could not diminish the popularity of
Thecla's story and the intrigue over this particular scripture
throughout the centuries.

These two human men in positions of exceptional spiritual
power and influence interpreted scripture in a way that validated how they saw women: as the lesser sex, the less divine
sex, as the sex that created sin, as the sex that is actually at fault
for human sin, as the sex that is opposite to their own—which
is closer to god, which is closer to the image of god "himself."

This reminds me of author and speaker Alok Vaid-Menon's
definition of power: "Power can be defined as the ability to
make a particular perspective seem universal."[7]

Saint Augustine was the first to write the phrase "original
sin," or in Latin, *peccatum originale.* Augustine, a human man,
with many egoic powers at work within the theology he would
create in his lifetime, a theology that stood on the shoulders of
Tertullian, sought to justify an exalted status of his sex through
the scapegoating of a gender other than his own.

The Gospel of Mary, though, before Augustine, before Tertullian, contained a vision that humanity is not born with sin embedded in our bones, passed down through the generations and stemming from the first woman. It is not original. It is created by us when we mistake the ego for the true self. It's when we're guided by the ego rather than the soul, or by fear instead of love.

Christ in *The Gospel of Mary* of course does not use the word "ego," but what Christ explains to Mary is that each and every human being is comprised of a soul and seven powers. These seven powers, which are modified and recast as "the seven deadly sins" hundreds of years later within Christianity, are aspects of our humanity that are not intrinsically "sinful." The judgment or description of them as "deadly sins" didn't begin until after the fourth century.

Within the context of the first and second century, these seven powers in *The Gospel of Mary* are simply that, powers. They affect our actions; they don't justify the horrible things we sometimes do, but they help us to understand why. And by becoming aware of the "why" behind our actions, we reclaim our capacity to choose what we do next.

Why did we honk and practically spit-swear at the car that cut us off? The seventh power is the power of wrath. Why did we eat seven Cronuts in a single day, or drink our weight in vodka this week? The fourth power is eagerness for death. Meaning excess. We as human beings often go all in. Not a handful of anything, but the whole bag. Not a small, manageable amount, but an extreme.

The Gospel of Mary doesn't see this, label it, and judge it as a "sin," but rather as a power. A power that's a part of what it means to be human. Our response is simply to see it, to become conscious of it, so we can have the chance to awaken while knee-deep in a power and make a different choice. Choose something new. Experience something else, something other than a slow, overwhelming extreme. So that maybe, eventually, we can experience an eagerness for life instead.

Or if we're not ready for what's next, we can experience the presence of curiosity rather than the shame and guilt the concept of sin conjures, as if these powers of wrath, excess, or desire prove we aren't good or worthy of goodness. Without the burden and weight the word "sin" imposes on us, we can have the spaciousness to be curious about why. Why are we going to these extremes?

Curiosity is the precursor to compassion, to mercy. And if we can be curious about a pattern we awaken to, we can also have the mercy on ourselves to seek help. If we're curious about our actions, rather than judgmental about what we do, we can hold on to that elusive and yet enduring truth that we're always worthy of reaching out our hand for a chance to change. If we let this concept of "sin," of being sinful innately, exist in us as a truth, then harmful actions and patterns in our lives will appear as if "proof" of this, rather than as powers of the ego. And we'll lose our grasp of knowing, remembering that we are always worthy of help, of mercy.

In the second chapter of *The Acts of Paul and Thecla*, a man named Onesiphorus looks for Paul with the help of a friend: "Titus had described Paul's appearance to him for he had not seen him in the flesh, but only in spirit" (2:1). Onesiphorus saw Paul "in spirit" before he saw him "in the flesh." This is the best way I can describe what I sensed about the word of god, before I found scriptures like *The Acts of Paul and Thecla* and *The Gospel of Mary*.

I sensed the presence of missing scripture long before I finally found it. I sensed maybe even that the spirit, if the spirit here refers to the feminine and the female presence in Christianity, was missing. And that this spirit, this presence, is also the word of god.

I'm curious about why my work of bringing to light the voices and scripture of the female figures within Christian history, as well as the feminine aspect of Christianity in the practice of going inward for contemplative prayer, is so threatening to some. That curiosity leads me to compassion. And that compassion helps me carry on. It connects me to something deeper than the words I am sometimes called for the work I do. Words like "animal," "witch," and my personal favorite, "whore."

I find it so curious that I am most often called the same word Mary Magdalene was labeled by the church from the sixth century onward. In almost two thousand years, this particular practice hasn't changed—that a woman in a place of spiritual authority, whether innate or earned or accrued through decades of study, is labeled a whore. As if that word had the power to render a woman somehow less powerful, or could delegitimize her teaching. I'm connected to a legacy of women throughout the centuries who have been labeled words meant to harm them, meant to "put them in their place," or shame and degrade them, but instead the name-calling lets us feel a common thread, as if to illuminate actual fire in the bloodstream, a DNA of dissent encoded within, unifying us throughout the generations.

A human being's proximity to the sacred has nothing to do with their sex or sexuality, or whether they've ever had sex or not. We'll return to this in chapter nine, "Purity."

For now, it's just critical to emphasize the amount of fear, rage, apprehension, and defensiveness I meet with when I suggest that the word of god wasn't compiled by god. What was eventually designated as the word of god was written, translated, and compiled by men. This is not my opinion; I am stating historical fact. A fact that is taught to every seminarian in the mandatory New Testament course that must be completed before graduation.

In a series of councils, beginning with the Council of Nicaea in 325 C.E., the canon law or official doctrine of the church, including the scripture that would be included in the New Testament, was decided by groups of bishops, starting with the one that Constantine ordered to meet for this purpose. Both the Catholic and the Eastern Orthodox churches recognize seven ecumenical, or universal, councils in the early centuries of the church, but Catholics also recognize fourteen additional councils that took place after the ninth century.

The first seven ecumenical councils are the Council of Nicaea in 325 C.E., the First Council of Constantinople in 381 C.E., the First Council of Ephesus in 431 C.E., the Council of Chalcedon in 451 C.E., the Second Council of Constantinople in 553 C.E., the Third Council of Constantinople from 680 to 681 C.E., and the Second Council of Nicaea in 787 C.E. All seven councils convened in what is now modern-day Turkey. Another meeting of bishops, which is not recognized as fully ecumenical, the Council of Rome in 382 C.E., compiled the first complete list of the scripture that had been deemed canonical.

It's important to name these councils because they exist— and yet they're so rarely taught as concrete evidence of the making and reshaping of a Christianity that established itself as orthodox. The aim of these councils was to reach a unified Christendom, which was ultimately established by inventing the concept of orthodoxy. To put it another way, in order to create a unified church beginning with Emperor Constantine in 325 C.E., councils of bishops decided which scriptures would henceforth be labeled apocryphal and which would become orthodox.

Constantine's agenda was not to represent the diversity of voices that existed in the myriad of scriptures within the Christ Movement; his agenda was to consolidate his empire. His agenda was to legitimate his reign with the word of god.

The deeply entrenched structure of power within the Roman Empire, the structure that placed the emperor at the top of a vertical axis, a hierarchy, from the fourth century onward was now given by divine decree. And inversely, those at the bottom of the axis of power, the women and slaves within the Roman Empire, were placed there not by human greed, not by injustice, not by the will of a powerful elite, but by god.

And so, the abundance of scripture that told another story about Christ, about power rather than sin, about what it means to be human, and about a love that liberates that's found within—all those scriptures that included the voices of women leaders, like *The Acts of Paul and Thecla* and *The Gospel of Mary*, were now considered heretical, unorthodox, and of "doubtful authenticity."

But as we know, rebellious monks wanted to keep these voices safe from erasure. They buried the scripture in caves and in urns like seeds in the Egyptian desert.

Just as the early church councils of the first six centuries decided which scripture from the Christ Movement would be excluded from the New Testament, the New Orleans Council of 2012, chaired by professor and pastor Hal Taussig, decided together which scriptures from the early Christ Movement, that have been unearthed over the past century, needed to be reintroduced to the traditional Christian canon, to form *A New New Testament*.

Unlike the early church councils, the New Orleans Council of 2012 consisted of nine women and ten men. The council was intentionally comprised of spiritual leaders from diverse backgrounds and experience. According to Taussig, the deliberations were "amiable, intense, and peppered with considerable disagreement."[8] Their common task in the discernment process was to give primary attention to the scripture that would provide the most spiritual value for the twenty-first century. The council was particularly drawn to scripture from the Christ Movement that had not been included in the New Testament that showed women in positions of leadership. Namely: *The Gospel of Mary, The Thunder: Perfect Mind, The Acts of Paul and Thecla,* and *The Diary of Perpetua.*

The Diary of Perpetua is considered the earliest surviving document written directly by a woman in leadership within the Christ Movement. However, it was composed in the third century, and the council wanted to include scripture written in the first or second century. Most estimates of *The Acts of Paul and Thecla* from the Greek composition of the scripture are mid-second century, but some scholars date it to as early as 70 C.E. So *The Acts of Paul and Thecla* was chosen over *The Diary of Perpetua* to be included in *A New New Testament.*

The Acts of Paul and Thecla was also chosen because Thecla clearly stands up to the Roman Empire and to the cultural expectations of women in the first century to claim her right to be a minister; her scripture therefore is clearly not patriarchal. It is evidence of a pre-patriarchal Christianity. The council added *The Acts of Paul and Thecla, The Thunder: Perfect Mind,* and *The Gospel of Mary* to create a shift in perception about commonly held assumptions of gender and power in the first centuries of Christianity.

In the end, the New Orleans Council reintroduced ten

more books to *A New New Testament:* "the Gospel of Mary, The Thunder: Perfect Mind, the Gospel of Thomas, the Odes of Solomon, the Prayer of Thanksgiving, the Acts of Paul and Thecla, the Gospel of Truth, the Prayer of the Apostle Paul, the Letter of Peter to Philip, and the Secret Revelation of John."[9]

What I find so curious is that an addition of more "word of god" could infuriate so many who see the New Testament as cast and created as if by god, as if fixed in time. When we know, empirically, that the New Testament was compiled over a series of centuries, and in the express interests of those who already held power.

I think the word of god is also this scripture that was originally cast out. I think the word of god includes those of us who speak truth to that same power that wants to assert itself again and again in every generation. That we might awaken to what has always also existed. The word of god according to someone with little to no power in the world around them. The word of god that includes her voice, not just his. The word of god that challenges our still to this day deeply entrenched gender roles in places of spiritual authority, just as it did in the first century.

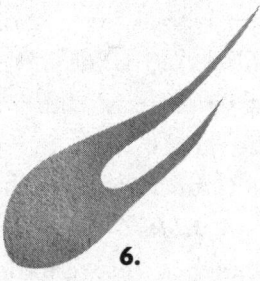

6.

Yes & No & Maybe

And he saw Paul coming—a man small in stature, with a bald head and crooked legs, healthy, with knitted eyebrows, a slightly long nose, and full of kindness—for at times he appeared as a human being and at others he had the face of an angel.

—The Acts of Paul and Thecla 3:2

The word "exegesis" comes from the Greek meaning "to interpret" or "out of," combined with "to guide or lead." Essentially, exegesis is just a strange theological term for interpretation. It's the critical process of uncovering the original or intended meaning of a passage of scripture.

The landscape of scripture for me as a theologian is not meant to be literal. And it's also real. Scripture is meant to be all things; it's metaphorical, allegorical, and symbolic. Scripture is sacred because it's meant to be read and interpreted as art. It's meant to serve as material for contemplation. To bring inward, like bits of kindling, to stoke a much less definable process of digesting the truth. A process that's intimate and personal. It's meant to break us out of our linear, binary thought patterns, our need to define and label and then subsequently delimit what scripture is telling us. It's meant to expand not only our thoughts but also the way we think.

The New Orleans Council unanimously agreed on including *The Thunder: Perfect Mind* into *A New New Testament,* primarily because gender in this scripture is both fluid and contradictory, or contradictory to binary thought. The only remaining copy of this scripture was found at Nag Hammadi in 1945. Its composition date has a wide range, from as early as the first century B.C.E. to potentially as late as the third century C.E. There's no indication of an author. However, its electrifying "I am" statements are more frequently from the feminine perspective—and describe the labels or roles more often expected of women. And what's most powerful, what has always gripped me every time I read it, is the way the voice in *The Thunder: Perfect Mind* simultaneously embodies what's considered sacred and profane.

> I am the first and the last
> I am she who is honored and she who is mocked
> I am the whore and the holy woman
> I am the wife and the virgin . . .
> I am the bride and the bridegroom . . .
> I am she, the lord . . .
> I am both awareness and obliviousness
> I am humiliation and pride
> I am without shame
> I am ashamed
> I am security and I am fear
> I am war and peace
> Pay attention to me

> I am she who is disgraced and she who is
>   important . . .
> I am what everyone can hear and no one can say[1]

When I interpret this scripture, it's more a state of being I enter into than any words or exegesis can fully capture. It's more this all-encompassing, ground-beneath-everything mind or space of heart I enter. If we look at the title of this scripture more closely, the word for "mind" in Greek is *nous,* but it doesn't refer to our modern concept of mind as an intellectual thought. "Mind" here doesn't mean what's opposite to the heart or to the vast spectrum of human emotions. "Mind" here is more closely akin to the heart's heart. *Nous* translates from the Greek as "the spiritual eye of the heart." So the perfect mind is more accurately a state of seeing from the heart, or a vision that love makes possible and that we can acquire from within. It's an ultimate power of discernment, a capacity to know—as if in the bones, or as in the Greek *gnosis,* meaning with direct experience—what is right, and true, and meant for us.

When I digest these "I am" statements in *The Thunder: Perfect Mind,* I become acutely aware that all our definitions, categories, labels, and names for ourselves and others have always been limited, confining, and ultimately incomplete. Incomplete because these identities lack the "and" between them. It's the whore or the holy woman, the wife or the virgin, humiliation or pride. The perfect mind here is when we reach a state of releasing this egoic concept of either-or, this egoic need to label and define those around us, and attempt to see from within, from a place that's not about control. From a place that's primarily about witnessing a love beneath it all, beneath every possible label and name we could call ourselves and one another—a love that holds and embodies every name that seeks to describe us.

I think *The Thunder* is meant to confuse the rational, linear mind, the egoic mind that defines, judges, and confines us and others all throughout the day, often without us even realizing. I think *The Thunder* wants us to hold "the opposites" together, to break our brains, to snap us out of that understandable and yet constraining mindset. I think more than telling a story, *The Thunder* is meant to teach us by asking us to enter a state of being, even if fleeting, where we can see all the "ands" that our humanity has always represented, the widest possible spectrum—the first *and* the last, the human *and* the angel, the virgin *and* the whore, the egoic self *and* the soul.

In *After Jesus Before Christianity,* scholars of the first hundred years of the Christ Movement explain that "women, and a significant number of men, rejected both male dominance and female passivity."[2] As a challenge to the traditional masculine/feminine and male/female dichotomies within the Roman Empire, the Christ Movement practiced a form of gender pluralism. So that the enculturated roles and expectations placed on men and women no longer applied to them.

What I wanted most to find in seminary was undeniable evidence that these scriptures recovered from the Christ Movement at Nag Hammadi confirm that Christ wanted to subvert the power structures of the Roman Empire, by extending his teachings to everyone—including women—and that therefore Christ was perhaps more radical and more radically loving than the later story of Jesus that formed within the institution of Christianity under Constantine from the fourth century onward.

I wanted a simple yes *or* no. Yes, this piece of scripture from antiquity proves that Christ is who you had hoped—a cross between a revolutionary minister and a Jewish social reformer, the love child of Dr. Martin Luther King, Jr., and Bernie Sanders. Or *no,* there just isn't enough evidence to know exactly who Christ was because he never wrote a word himself.

Instead, Professor Taussig had a magnificent and infuriating way of slapping me across the ego, like Cher in *Moonstruck* when Nicolas Cage's character says he loves her. When I began to take scripture too literally, when I clung to an aspect of the text as evidence that my personal belief in Christ was right and was now validated, he would respond to my need for confirmation with "Yes and no and maybe." And he'd say it slowly, so it would really sink in. So I could hear Gloria Steinem's famous maxim as if over a loudspeaker inside me: "The truth will set you free, but first it will piss you off."

My ego always felt the sting. And also, it felt like such a relief, every time I was knocked back into my heart, to remember I don't actually know anything for certain. Remembering this always feels like swapping from high heels to flats. None of us know empirical truths when it comes to theology, to god. That's not the point. The point is to question, wonder, and share what we know to be true with humility, and with the aim to strengthen love's reach.

Readers of my book *Mary Magdalene Revealed* often write to me and ask, "Do you think Christ and Mary were married?" And I offer the same brain-breaking response Professor Taussig used to give me: "Yes and no and maybe."

Yes, there is scripture that indicates they had a unique and exceptional relationship. For example, in *The Gospel of Mary,* Peter says to Mary Magdalene, "Sister, we know that the Savior loved you more than all other women" (6:1).[3] And because of this love, Christ shares secret teachings with Mary that he wanted her to then share with the disciples. In *The Gospel of Philip*, Mary is described as the *koinonos* of Christ, which translates from the Greek as "partner" or "companion," and the gospel says "he often kissed her on the mouth."[4]

And no, we don't have any irrefutable evidence to point to (today, at least) that proves they were married. And maybe it makes sense that Christ would have been married, as the ancient proverb relates, "that which is not lived is not redeemed."[5]

In *The Acts of Paul and Thecla*, as Onesiphorus watches Paul approach for the first time in chapter three, "at times he appeared as a human being and at others he had the face of an angel" (3:2). When we read this now, we can see the importance of the "and." Paul appears as a human *and* an angel, both. So, we can see that he is both a central figure, a saint even, in this early Christ Movement, and also, simultaneously, he's a human man who both wants to practice the gender pluralism of the Christ Movement and perhaps also wants to keep the power he experiences as a man within the Roman Empire. He wants to empower the women around him, and he also struggles with what that will mean for him.

What "yes and no and maybe" gives us is the most powerful stance, or state of mind, we can enter as we encounter scripture—a state of mind that means seeing from the heart, a heart that holds all the possible answers as the ground beneath it.

It's brain-breaking, I know. But our modern definition and understanding of mind—our thoughts, our consuming ticker tape of egoic thoughts—has only gotten us so far. Many, most, would say we are in desperate need for a new way of seeing in the world. So we can discern new answers. *The Thunder: Perfect Mind* points us back to an original "mind." A vision that allows us to embrace the human and the angel in us both. In *The New York Times,* author and illustrator Mira Jacob writes:

> At night when I am my most panicked, I find myself trying to evolve in real time, to grow the part that will change us faster. That sounds like a metaphor. It's not. What if a body that's lived more years than it has left under a colonialist, capitalist, white patriarchy carries the potential for our better future, specifically the as yet untapped ability to grow a new organ that will recognize how deeply our futures are intertwined, allowing us to reach our full potential by finally bridging the gap between our limited imaginations and our collective survival.[6]

What if we already contain this "new organ"? What if there's no need to wait to grow it; what if it just has, through millennia of atrophy from disuse, been forgotten? What if it's this "mind," this eye of the heart, this faculty of insight that can hold the extremes of humanity, our brutality and our redivivus love, to lead us to what we haven't known before? What if it's just as simple and profound as the myths and legends have always tried to tell us, that the treasure we seek far and wide for has been buried all along in our own backyard?

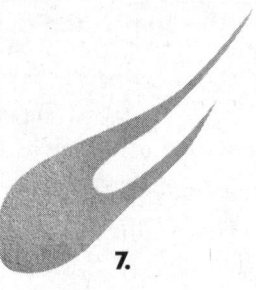

7.

Voice

And when Paul saw Onesiphorus, he smiled and Onesiphorus said, "Welcome, servant of the blessed God!" And Paul replied, "Grace to you and your household!" But Demas and Hermogenes were jealous and went further into their hypocrisy so that Demas said, "Are we not of the Blessed, too, that you all have not welcomed us just as him?"

—*The Acts of Paul and Thecla* (4:1–2)

Theologians in the past have traditionally written with an omniscient voice when interpreting scripture, not locating what they say in the body that's writing it. As if to write and speak of divine and esoteric things, we need to somehow deny the human reality of being in a body, thereby diminishing and erasing all the ways that particular embodiment shapes how we interpret scripture. *The Gospel of Philip,* an ancient text also found at Nag Hammadi, reminds us, "What you say, you say in a body. You can say nothing outside this body. You must awaken while in this body, for everything exists in it: Resurrect in this life."[1]

I can say nothing outside this small white female body. And this statement is not meant to be reductionist or essentialist. It comes from an awareness that my physical reality shapes what I encounter, how I am treated, and what is expected of me. It's awareness of privileged access and treatment I've experienced throughout my life because of my skin, and also assault and misogyny I've endured because of my sex. And it's awareness of the limits and dangers of heteronormative language because my sexuality exists as a spectrum, not a fixed point. Or, to quote David Rose, Dan Levy's character from *Schitt's Creek,* "I like the wine, not the label."

My voice is sewn into the sinews of this body. I see and hear aspects of scripture that someone else in a body unlike mine might not. My physical reality shapes my metaphysical beliefs. And this is why it's so critical to hear from as many voices as possible, to hear the truth of our diverse experience, and how that informs our ideation of the divine.[2] We need more theologies devoted to being present in the body rather than the antiquated spiritual ideal of claiming authority by transcending it.

Who gets to translate scripture? Only the trained? Only the ordained? Of course not. It's anyone who feels called to. It's anyone who believes in their voice enough not to silence it.

Demas and Hermogenes will soon betray Paul and Thecla, so they're a hard-to-love duo in this story. But here, before the drama unfolds, they ask, "Are we not of the Blessed, too?" (4:2). And it's a good question. They weren't originally invited, but that question, the fact that they speak up and ask it, gets them through the door.

It lands for any one of us who has felt excluded, somehow left out, and not considered "blessed" enough to be given a proverbial seat at the table, or a welcome once we get across the threshold.

For almost two millennia, the predominant voice interpreting scripture has been from the body of a male, and in the

West, a white male. That is the predominant voice that has been shared, that has been published and given a platform, and that has been vested with the authority of the church. For almost two millennia, we've had a predominant lived experience sharing a story about god that came from a position of privilege, and of power.

When feminist poet Audre Lorde was preparing to deliver a paper on the topic of transforming silence into language, her daughter Elizabeth said to her:

> Tell them about how you're never really a whole person if you remain silent, because there's always that one little piece inside that wants to be spoken out, and if you keep ignoring it, it gets madder and madder and hotter and hotter, and if you don't speak it out one day it will just up and punch you in the mouth from the inside.[3]

When Lorde delivered her paper, she warned everyone listening, "Your silence will not protect you."[4] And she asked her audience to consider, "What are the words you do not yet have? What do you need to say?"[5]

Is silence a virtue? Really? Maybe silence is only a virtue to those who have always had the power to speak, to be heard, and to be believed. Maybe silence is not a virtue, though, for those of us who have been silenced.

Maybe the only silence that's virtuous is the silence we can find within us, the peace that comes once we've found a way to express "that one little piece inside that wants to be spoken out."

In her groundbreaking feminist book *Heart of Flesh*, Benedictine nun and theologian Sister Joan Chittister writes about the symbolic evidence of women's invisibility and erasure with the use of exclusively male pronouns, terminology, and prayers about "brotherhood" and "brethren," as if those prayers are somehow meant to speak to all of us. She asks, "What happens to the spiritual life of a young girl who is made to understand, consciously or subconsciously, that she has no place in the spiritual domain except as a consumer of someone else's *god*?"[6]

Her work inspired me to think about the fact that spiritual practices have not been created with women in mind. Women's embodied reality has never been factored into what it even means to be spiritual. For example, a monk's rigorous spiritual day of silence, selfless service, emphasis on love and the emotional support of others, and denial of the body, with extra sacred bonus points for skipping meals—this is a typical secular Tuesday for most women. It's both aggravating and inspiring to consider the depth of women's omission. To think about how so many of us are participating in a spiritual framework that was intentionally created to never include us.

Meeting Sister Joan Chittister was my version of meeting the pope. She is my popess. (Autocorrect can't seem to figure out what I'm trying to write, and keeps turning the word "popess" back to "pope.") Author and activist V (formerly Eve Ensler) invited me to give a TEDxWomen talk with her titled "The Rising." I met Sister Joan right before I was about to go onstage. Her exuberance was blinding. She said something that was reassuring, and I nodded, dazed. But I couldn't hear her actual words—the strength of those beams of light streaming out of her eyes overpowered my ability to take anything else in. All I could do was listen to her light. And I took it with me onstage as I used my voice in public for the first time to talk about how our ideas of the divine directly affect the status of women. And how recovering the voice of the divine feminine in world religions as a scholar helped me also to personally recover my own.

It was seven of the most intense minutes of my life, up there onstage, being filmed before this live audience. Trying not to trip on these weirdly long red pants I was wearing, and trying not to forget to just stay in my body, stay present, to speak from the love that led me there to begin with. Sister Joan was way up in the balcony to my left. I couldn't see her past this glaring spotlight placed at the foot of the stage, but I felt those beams of light from her eyes even still.

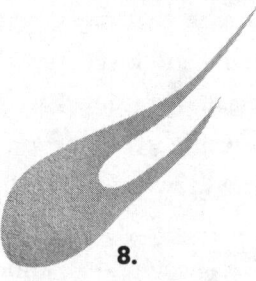

8.

Power

And Onesiphorus said, "I do not see in you the fruits of justice, but if you are anything, come to my house as well and rest."

—*The Acts of Paul and Thecla* 4:3

The fruits of justice.

This phrase names something for me. It makes visible or points to a capacity we all share to "see" what is ineffable and invisible and yet no less real in another person's face, or maybe mostly the eyes. As if the kindness Paul possesses and the love he has cultivated from his storytelling about Christ is somehow discernible. As if the inner work, that quiet, lonely effort of becoming more love, can be seen.

As a feminist theologian, I have to imagine a world that doesn't exist yet. Or it exists, but just in moments of kindness between us, or in collaborations that work to end injustice, or in gatherings of even just a very few people, when we make visible together this truth that every human being is created equally to be recognized and loved.

The first time I felt as if that inner world I can imagine was met tangibly in the outside world, or said again, the first time I felt I was finally sitting down in a church I belonged to, I was in a philosophy course in divinity school.

Dr. Cornel West stood behind an antique-looking wooden lectern and spoke in a way that made the phrase "the word of god" actually make sense to me. My soul seemed to lurch to full attention each time he preached. I mean, taught. He referred to us as brothers and sisters, as siblings. He spoke to us of unconditional love, of the radical love, Christ is for him. And he illuminated the ways that we are called to put that love into practice.

The horseshoe-shaped room had curved, wooden pews with descending platforms down to where Dr. West stood. And this became my sanctuary. A wooden womb. I inherited something with each next lecture. I felt called. I felt inspired. Because the church I thought I would only experience within me was for moments right here, tangible and present, in his teaching.

The whole class clapped at the end of his lectures. And my friend, let's call him Candle-man, and I would often initiate a standing ovation. Candle-man was a law student, and we met for the first time, oddly enough, not on campus in Cambridge but during winter break back in Cleveland. He was carrying a candle the first time I saw him.

The midnight Christmas Eve ceremony at the First Unitarian Church of Cleveland was my only remaining exposure to church after walking out of it as a little girl. We went because my mom loved the candle ceremony. It starts with all of us sitting in the dark together with the lights off in the sanctuary, and with each of us holding a small unlit candle that has this cute paper skirt to catch falling wax. Then there's the sudden, striking contrast of a flash from a single candle being lit. And gradually, bit by patient bit, all throughout the sanctuary, the light is restored, as we carefully pass that initial flame from wick to wick.

Candle-man thanked me with a nod, as I held the door open for him while he sheltered his candle with his hand. And I stood there, probably with my mouth open, staring. As I watched him carry his small flame from out of the church and into the storm, I said one of those desperate prayers I would become more familiar with and more responsible for in the years to come. I vowed, or wagered really, that if I could just see him again, I would devote my life to god.

The actual words I used, though, which I cringe at now, but the words that came to me in the urgency of the moment, were that I vowed to become "a voice piece of love." A voice piece? Who says that? Where did that even come from? But I felt the impact of having declared it within me; it felt as if I had signed a binding contract as I watched Candle-man's car pull out of the church parking lot. Not knowing who he was, where he was headed, or if I would ever see him again.

A few weeks later, back in Cambridge on campus, we crossed paths at an intersection. My heart was beating hard enough to break my ribs. I was in shock, I think. I felt this torrent flash of anxiety. I have no idea what I said to him, some version of "hello" or "what the hell." Whatever I said, it stopped him from walking past me. He stared at me with that confused look of recognizing me but not knowing why. I managed past my awkwardness enough to explain that I was the one who had held the church door open for him back in Cleveland.

This is when I found out Candle-man's real name, and this is when he suggested I join him in Dr. West's philosophy course. Candle-man loved John Coltrane's *A Love Supreme.* Which I listened to a lot that winter. And we fell in love, a little bit. Mostly, though, our meeting was about that candle he was holding, and the clarity I began to feel about what I was called to do because we met. Or because of how we met the second time. Our relationship and Dr. West's sermons allowed me to become more acutely aware of power. True power. And where true power rests.

We were sitting at a jazz club in downtown Boston when it finally sunk in. He had gone to the bar to get us two Manhattans (which I didn't even like, but I liked the idea that we could drink the same drink), and I went to get us one of those tiny two-person tables with the circular tops. There was only one free, so I sat down, and then noticed this slip of paper that had been left there. I picked it up and read the small message written across it: "Be Careful What You Wish For."

My cheeks flushed. It felt as though I were being held accountable for what I did. Secretly, silently, I had made that wager with god. More accurately, I had held god by the collar, with more of a demand than a prayer, to see Candle-man again. And we both knew, but hadn't named it yet by the time I read the warning, that we were friends primarily, not lovers or partners.

I will never forget that moment of seeing him for the first time, how it was more a sense of recognizing him. Or of seeing in him "the fruits of justice" that were right there, discernible just beneath the skin. And I will never forget the moment of seeing him for the second time, how I felt this rush of magic, this surge of power that came from within me but that was so much more than me. It left pure awe in its wake.

And I will never forget those moments of sitting beside him in Dr. West's class and feeling these rivulets of joy, these shivers of chill-fire race through me, as Dr. West spoke about a world of love I had only ever encountered, privately, within. Alone.

There was a power in me he was speaking to directly, a power I had misplaced, a power I had been severed from, a power I had projected onto others, a power I had siphoned away bit by bit my entire life.

There was a power in me Dr. West's words made visceral. A power that was far more than I could ever be individually. A power we've rarely practiced or seen in action. A power *with*. Not a power *over* another, a power shared. A power we are learning to call love.

Over a decade later, I felt that now familiar surge of presence and heat when my soul suddenly slams up against the back of my face, as I read a *Times* article on October 13, 2014, that began, "Author, activist, and academic Cornel West was arrested Monday in Ferguson, Mo., amid continued demonstrations demanding justice for Mike Brown, the unarmed black teenager who was killed by a white police officer Aug. 9."

I quickly googled Dr. West and Ferguson. A video came to the top of the screen. I clicked on it. Dr. West was linked arm in arm, forming a human chain, with other faith leaders peacefully demanding justice for Mike Brown's murder.

Then there's a face-off between the human chain of spiritual leaders and armed police officers. An officer grabs Dr. West, forcefully pulls his arms so that they are pinned behind his back. Then he presses Dr. West down with all his weight until he is on his knees, and then until his face, radiant with justice, is nearly touching the cement beneath him.

I'm often asked: Are you a theologian or an activist? As if theology and politics could ever be or have ever been separate.

To be a theologian, for me, is to be called to tell the truth about love. As Dr. West explained in a post on Twitter in 2010, "To be a Christian is to live dangerously, honestly, freely—to step in the name of love as if you may land on nothing, yet to keep on stepping because the something that sustains you no empire can give you and no empire can take away."

What I thought was my first experience of falling in love, of love at first sight even, was actually my first real taste of true power. The power I called on from within me, in that desperate, cringe-worthy prayer, to see Candle-man again. Not knowing that I already attended the same graduate school as he did, not knowing that the light that he was holding, the light that I was actually following, was leading me to a love story much larger than my own.

9.

Purity

Paul said, "Blessed are the clear of heart, for they will see God."

—*The Acts of Paul and Thecla* 5:1

P aul enters Onesiphorus's house and with "great joy" they kneel, break bread, and talk about what it means to be blessed. If you're familiar with the Sermon on the Mount in Matthew 5, it sounds a lot like Paul's remake version of that, except it's the Sermon on Onesie's Floor.

If you don't know the Sermon on the Mount, Matthew 5 goes a little bit like this: "Blessed are those who hunger and thirst for justice, for they will be satisfied. Blessed are the merciful, for they will find mercy. Blessed are the pure in heart, for they will see God."[1]

Paul's remake version in *The Acts of Paul and Thecla* begins with nearly the exact same words that Christ ends his sermon with in Matthew 5: "Blessed are the clear of heart, for they will see God." Except Paul says "clear" of heart where Matthew says "pure." Paul, like Christ's sermon in Matthew, then launches into a litany of "Blessed ares." And many of Paul's "Blessed ares" focus on the purity, or rather chastity, of the female body.

Paul says, "Blessed are those that have wives as if they do not, for they will be heirs of God" (5:5).[2] A critical reality becomes visible with this one statement. First, Paul is revealing that although he may have allowed men and women to sit equally beside him and listen, he is only addressing the men, "those that have wives." The subject here is "those" that have wives, and the object is the "wives."

I have to imagine this was an awkward moment for Onesie. After all, we know from chapters one through four that he has a wife and a family. Clearly, he has been with his wife "as a wife." It must have been even more awkward for Onesie's wife, Lectra. Here she is kneeling on the floor with this short, sometimes angelic-looking bald man, after she has welcomed him into her home, and he reveals in this statement that he's not actually even talking to her; he's addressing her husband about no longer being with her sexually in order to somehow be closer to god.

Purity makes my blood boil for one fundamental reason: Purity has been predominantly defined by men in positions of power since antiquity. According to Linda Kay Klein, author of *Pure,* "The term 'purity culture' is generally associated with the white, American, Evangelical Christian Purity Movement and the corollary Purity Industry launched in the early 1990s."[3] In reality, the concept of purity and its gender-based sexual control spans religions and cultures throughout the world. A prevailing outcome of purity culture is that males are taught their *thoughts* are pure or impure, whereas females are taught that their *bodies* are pure or impure.

And purity, from the male perspective in antiquity, dropped anchor with this one lasting idea that it pertains to heteronormative sex, whether it's consensual or not. And that the responsibility for proving this "purity" falls exclusively on one party: women and girls.

If Paul had let Lectra give us a sermon on what it meant to be pure in Iconium in the first century, I have to imagine her idea of purity might have expanded to include the body. As a mother, she may have experienced—as I have experienced—that holy interstice of what's truly sacred and profoundly human that giving birth demands.

Paul declares, "Blessed are the bodies of maidens"—not the maidens themselves, mind you, but their virginal bodies— "for they will have favor with God and will not lose the reward for their holiness" (6:7).[4] So, for maidens, their holiness relies on their inexperience with heteronormative sex. Their holiness is in their bodies. But only if they don't actually enjoy, explore, or experience the power their bodies contain. Their holiness is controlled then by the ones who wield the power to define and bestow this holiness on them. Or, said again, their holiness relies on the amount of power they give over for others to define and delimit their purity and what constitutes it.

This takes me back to the way that Paul says "clear" where Matthew says "pure." "Blessed are the clear of heart, for they will see god." For me, the word "clear" is free of the weight and history "purity" wields. What I mean is, I think purity has to do with the clarity of our own heart. And no one outside of us has any say in either the inner work it takes for us to get clear, or what the outcome looks like in being "pure."

So, let me restate what makes my blood boil about Paul's statement on maidens and the idea that their purity hinges on their virginity. Purity has to do with a state we enter, an alignment with our truth, a fierce authenticity with what our heart compels us to do. This is true power.

When someone defines for us that we can only be pure if . . . that's taking power away. It's taking our capacity to define, to know, and to speak our own truth about what being pure means for us.

If we even care about the currency of that idea at all.

Many of us do not have the possibility, or the privilege, of having complete control over what happens to our bodies. I am a survivor. And I know that one in three women, one in six men, and almost half of all transgender people will experience sexual violence in their lifetimes, according to the World Health Organization. And I know that human trafficking is a global, multibillion-dollar industry.

And every one of us is holy.

Purity cannot be established outside of us; it cannot be proven or tested or conferred upon us. Holiness is so much more unconditional than that. I have to imagine that if all those within the Roman Empire who did not have control over their own bodies would have been a part of defining what purity meant theologically from the start, it would have had to do with the heart.

Blessed are the clear of heart, for they will see god.

The Gospel of Mary reveals that there are seven powers of the ego that are contained within each of us as aspects of our humanity. And these seven powers are a part of what it means to be a "true human," or *anthropos,* from the Greek, which translates as "fully human and fully divine." The other half of what it means to be human is to be a soul.

The seven powers that Christ reveals to Mary in her gospel, which we each contain (in a wild assortment of degrees), are darkness, desire, ignorance, eagerness for death, the realm of the flesh, the foolish wisdom of the flesh, and wrathful wisdom (9:16–25).[5]

The point here, in being human, is not to avoid or deny the experience of any one of these seven powers; the point is to keep remembering when we're entrenched, neck deep in the emotions and feelings these powers create, that we are also a soul.

What does that mean?

When we remember we are not only this temporary (however compelling and powerful) compulsion of wrath, while we are actually in the messy, sweaty grip of it, we can bring love to where it hasn't been before. We can practice being fully human, the *anthropos*.

This practice is called *anamnesis,* or "living remembrance." The work is ongoing, never perfect, just persistent. The work is to remember that in the midst of the worst that can happen in our life, we are also, miraculously, humanly, a soul. Both-and, not either-or.

Similar to the Buddhist meditation practice of "no-self," the people of the Christ Movement practiced *kenosis,* which translates as "self-emptying love," and *The Gospel of Mary* might be proof of the origin of that contemplative practice. I say "might" because we only have three fragments of her gospel, so scholars have to draw from what remains.

Mary relates a vision she had of Christ in her gospel. And she asks him in the vision to explain how she is able to "see" or perceive him directly from within. Christ answers her, "Blessed are you that you did not waver at seeing me. For where the mind is, there is the treasure" (7:3–4).[6] Then Mary asks him, which I love her for, because she's not afraid to roll down the window and ask for detailed directions, "Lord, now, does one who sees a vision see it with the soul or with the spirit?" (7:5).[7] And Christ responds, "One does not see with the soul or with the spirit, but the mind which is between the two sees the vision" (7:6–7).[8] Christ's response is abruptly cut off here, because the rest of chapter seven and all of chapter eight in *The Gospel of Mary* are missing.

Her gospel resumes abruptly in the middle of chapter nine with what seems to be a dialogue between the soul and the seven powers. So, we as readers have to interpret for ourselves what Christ's full answer might have been. We have to figure out for ourselves why Christ refers to "the mind" as "the treasure," knowing as we do that "mind" here comes from the Greek word *nous,* meaning "the spiritual eye of the heart." And that it's this spiritual eye within us that is able to perceive a vision, to discern what's true. Maybe the seven powers are mentioned after Mary's question because these egoic powers are what can cloud and confuse our spiritual perception.

Since all three fragments of *The Gospel of Mary* are missing these same pages, it may have been the most incendiary teaching her gospel contains. After all, if Mary can perceive directly from within her what is true and real, then no one can control her, or mislead her into believing, for example, that she's unworthy of leadership or spiritual authority simply because she's female.

When Paul, or the mystics, or other saints I adore within the church, talk about seeing god, I used to assume that when such a sighting happens, that's it. THE END. DONE. GAME OVER. I see god and then *boom,* I never act human again. I just walk around like a monk in a red dress.

What I never really understood until I started practicing a

form of *kenosis* myself is that forever, the infinite, god, the love that liberates, is outside of time. It can be experienced right here within my tiny finite body, but it exists outside of time. And if I can see it, come face-to-face with it, I get to experience what's timeless even as the seconds continue to race by. What doesn't survive is my idea of myself, or the bramble of egoic powers I was caught up in.

So, when Paul declares in his sermon on Onesie's floor, "Blessed are the clear of heart, for they will see God," and if Mary's gospel is restored to our comprehension of Christ's teachings, I hear him saying blessed are the ones who do the work of remembering the other half of what it means to be human. Blessed are the ones who feel all the hard, horrible, and painful things in being human, and still find their way back, again and again, to love. Blessed are the ones who know that everything that happens to us is material for our own liberation.

The story about Christ that began to be institutionalized as orthodox Christianity in the fourth century—what Harvard scholar Dr. Karen King refers to as "the master story"—enshrined god as the father, and the father only. This is the story that perpetuates the justification of an exclusively male succession of divine authority.

It also perpetuates this outdated arrangement: Since the male is the carrier of all that's divine—the word of god, Christ's gender, and the exclusive sex to receive transmission of authority within the church for the majority of the past two millennia—then the female is the carrier of sexuality, of purity, of the weight of the word and status "virginal," and of the weight of the word and status "whore."

Armed with this "master story," beginning in the fourth century, women were edited and erased from positions of authority within the Christian story. Mary of Nazareth, Christ's mother, by 431 C.E. at the Council of Ephesus, would be declared *Theotokos,* God-bearer, immaculate, removing the "sin" of sex from Mary, and placing her in such an impossibly exalted state of virginity that no human woman could identify with her or draw strength from the fact that Mary physically gave birth to Christ.

Mary Magdalene's image would undergo the opposite transformation from "Mary the Immaculate Virgin." She would be declared by Pope Gregory in the sixth century as the penitent prostitute.[9] And this fictitious narrative about Mary, about both Marys, would serve to justify why women were innately unfit for positions of spiritual authority. And the virgin/whore dichotomies would affect religious and secular women from antiquity to the modern age.

What this successfully erased over the next two millennia was evidence of the female counterparts, or companions, to the central male figures in the history of Christianity. Christ lost Mary Magdalene. And Paul the Apostle lost his counterpart, Thecla. We lost the voice, the unique courage, and the wisdom of what it meant for a woman to reclaim her spiritual authority at a time when women had little to no power over their bodies much less their lives.

I rewatched (binge-watched, that is) *Buffy the Vampire Slayer* during the strange and isolating months of the COVID-19 pandemic. And at some point, as I was making my way through the spin-off show, *Angel,* a character named Cordelia said, "If a male body was needed for sacrifice and holiness, the world would be atheist just like that."

What Cordelia illuminates here is that the entire concept of holiness as it relates to the female body doesn't actually have anything to do with "purity" or "virginity" at all. It has to do with dominance. It has to do with power.

Because a girl, a woman, a wife, a mother who cares about purity, who sees purity as inextricably linked to her value in the world, to her actual worth within it, is then controlled by it.

Religious scholars and historians who have written about *The Acts of Paul and Thecla* have focused on Thecla's refusal to marry as a spiritual imperative for purity. I suspect, though, that Thecla's refusal to marry might also have everything to do with power, and how she went about answering a call that came from within her at a time when she wasn't free to do so. Her refusal to marry might have had more to do with her way of reclaiming control over her own body than adherence to a patriarchal rendering of purity. By refusing to marry, her body was no longer her father's possession to give in marriage to her husband, and for her husband to then own by law.

Thecla's story electrified me when I first read it in seminary. It felt like the most personally relevant and liberating piece of scripture I had ever encountered. Because even though I had remained on the periphery of any Christian community, even though I had been raised in a quasi-agnostic family by a card-carrying feminist, getting indoctrinated into the misogyny of Christianity doesn't require attendance in church.

Here's what I mean. When I was Thecla's age, at seventeen, there was this sexy (to me, because smart) young man who was a senior when I was a junior in high school. His name in Hebrew translates as "the listener," and everyone I knew thought the listener was *it*. So, when he told me that he liked me and wanted to date me, I felt this pressure as if I'd been chosen. As if I'd won the lottery without even buying a ticket. My "yes" felt assumed, a given.

This is how I soon found myself in the listener's basement with his tongue in my ear. And since I have zero poker-face capacity, my expression in the dark was an award-winning reenactment of Munch's *The Scream*. So even though my face was telling the truth, I was pretending to enjoy his bizarre exploration of my inner ear with fake moans that I had learned from *Dirty Dancing*.

Later that night, as I was driving back home from the listener's house, I couldn't stop crying. He had asked me to prom, so I felt like I should have been happy, or at least felt good that he had asked me. But I felt miserable. And at the time, I couldn't understand why.

I had never once considered if I liked him. I was the one he had chosen, but I had never actually chosen him. I didn't understand myself to be in a position to choose. And I didn't even have the words at that time to see any of this. I was not my own. I was not the subject of my own story. I was complacent in being the object of his.

The listener asked after we had sex for the first time (my first, not his) if I felt different now that I had "lost" my virginity to him. I was so perplexed at the sexist math. I had somehow lost worth by having sex, and he had miraculously gained it. But I didn't express any of this. I just smiled slightly and looked at him as though I didn't understand. Perpetuating this inexplicable deception of who I was, of what I wanted, and of what I already knew. But why? What was I so afraid of?

Humiliating him. Inciting his rage at my rejection. Breaking entrenched cultural expectations that I reciprocate if a young man likes me—that I am somehow responsible for his desire. I can see now that these were unspoken forces that affected my sense of personal agency, but I couldn't back then.

The relationship ended a couple of years later when the listener moved to Israel to join a Hasidic community. I still remember holding the letter he sent to my dorm in college to explain his decision, where he referred to me as "the forbidden fruit." Though that wasn't the part that upset me. I didn't mind that description. Still don't. Has a ring to it. What was most upsetting was not the way the relationship ended, but that it ever started to begin with.

The complete inability for me to see, to know, to act on my own power, my own choices; this is what would disturb me most in the years to come, which would contain long stretches of times when, like Thecla, I chose to be my own.

And what disturbed me even more over the years was seeing how profoundly universal it is. This lack of awareness or this inability among other girls and women I know that we get to say "no" to anyone or anything we don't want. That we are not commodities. That our lives don't have to be consumed with finding a partner. That we don't have to pin our worth on any aspect of our status as a female, not as a wife, mother, sister, daughter. Never. None of it. Worth is innate, not earned, proven, or bought. Worth is claimed.

We don't ever have to say yes out of the pervasive shadow of male violence. We can always refuse to be who someone else needs us to be. And also, some of us were silenced before we could even use the word. "No" is the greatest luxury that so many today, right now, can't say, or at least can't say without costing them their lives.

Maybe, just as Paul was claiming the female body as blessed and most holy only when untouched, Lectra was simultaneously whispering a litany of what was most blessed to her.

Blessed are the outcasts, the forgotten, the terrified, the silenced, for they will find the voice of love inside them. Blessed are those who wear only what the soul desires, for they will recognize one another and never walk alone.

THE SECOND STAGE

Some stories create a metamorphic shift in perception, a new way of seeing ourselves, our lives, the otherworldly worth of it, and what we'll do with the brief time we have here to live it. That's the second stage: a new way of seeing what might be possible for us. As if a door opens that we never even noticed was there.

10.

Worth

A certain maiden, Thecla—whose mother was Theocleia and was promised in marriage to a man, Thamyris—sat at a window close to the house and listened night and day to the message about holiness spoken by Paul. She did not turn away from the window, but moved forward in faith, rejoicing exceedingly. And yet having seen many women and maidens coming to Paul, she also desired for herself to be deemed worthy, to stand face-to-face with Paul and hear the word of Christ.

—*The Acts of Paul and Thecla* 7:1–2

We are introduced to Thecla first as "a certain maiden." The English word "maiden" comes from the Old English *mægden*, which is a Germanic diminutive of "maid, virgin," or "unmarried woman." Her introduction then in this scripture, the first descriptor used to define Thecla, implicates her in an economy of worth that has to do with her body as a commodity.

It's significant to tear open this initial description of Thecla, because in many ways it defines the rest of her story; it's the most powerful reality she fights to overcome. And the challenges she will have to face all originate from that one descriptor: She is seen by the world around her foremost for her worth as a maiden. She is not Thecla, a person, a human with unforeseen potential; she's Thecla, a girl who can be leveraged by her family for wealth and power through marriage. The primary expectation of Thecla boils down to this word "maiden," meaning virgin.

What causes such a world-shattering shift in her community is that Thecla opts out of this economy of worth that she is born into. Thecla refuses to be a commodity. She refuses to do what is innately expected of her because her sole worth according to the world around her is tethered to her reproductive potential, which has value to those who see themselves as owning her and as having the right then to force her to do what they expect.

I don't know how long it will take, or what it will take to see the day when a child can be a child, when a soul can grow into defining what is meant for them, what is authentic to them. The day when nothing is expected or presumed of us simply based on our sex or gender. The day when our worth is seen as intrinsic, just for being human. When our worth doesn't come from what we can provide or produce. When our worth is inherent. When our existence alone merits worth.

It's significant to see here in this ancient scripture, which could date back to as early as the first century, Thecla introduced as a maiden. Then within that same chapter, we see that Thecla "desired for herself to be deemed worthy, to stand face-to-face with Paul." This is the detrimental impact of the economy of worth Thecla was born into as a female. She has to deem herself worthy of such proximity to Paul. She must go on an internal journey, a struggle; a healing has to happen before she can allow herself to approach him.

This is unique to those of us who have felt the weight of the economy of worth that sees us as foremost a body, a commodity. We have to build a bridge between what we desire and what we feel worthy of having. This is what I witness in Thecla's story. Thecla's worth has only ever been tethered to an external expectation of what she will do with her body for her family's sake, but Paul's words have unmoored her, so now she reaches for a worth that has absolutely nothing to do with what others expect of her.

I think worth is the key to seeing new possibilities for what life we are capable of experiencing. And it's so ferociously elusive. To feel worthy. To know we are worthy. To have a sense of self-worth. For many of us with trauma, that path to reclaiming a sense of our innate worthiness can be treacherous and hard-won. It's elusive because we often imagine it will be given to us by someone else, that it will be accrued through acts of service or through external achievements. But our worthiness in being human is deeper and more hidden than anything we can actually point to, earn, or prove, and anything that could in the end be taken from us.

There is a Black Madonna in France in a small town called Besse, which I visited the summer before entering theological studies. When the tour guide began to give the group of pilgrims I was with a brief history about this particular Black Madonna, he mentioned that she had a reliquary in her back. There was a small, almost imperceptible wooden door on the back of the statue, and within was a shallow little closet where relics were kept. The tour guide went on to share more history about her, but I remained right there, with that image he'd created, with the sudden discovery of a secret little storage unit behind my heart. Because that's where I felt my sense of self-worth was held. In the shadow of my heart. In the center of my back, behind a door I could barely reach, and in a space I would never be able to see.

There are three truths I know about it: I did not put it there. No one, and no circumstance, can take it from me. And when I sense it, there like a real thing, like an actual relic held safe behind my heart, I remember that I have no idea just how much I might be worthy of in my short life. Because whatever I might imagine from my limited egoic mind is most likely a fragment of what is actually possible, and a fraction of what I am actually worthy of receiving.

It's fascinating that the phrase "face-to-face" is here in our first encounter with Thecla: "she also desired for herself to be deemed worthy, to stand face-to-face with Paul." As soon as I first read this passage decades ago in *The Acts of Paul and Thecla*, I thought of Paul's well-known sermon from 1 Corinthians 13: "As yet we see, in a mirror, dimly, but then— face-to-face! As yet my knowledge is incomplete, but then I will know in full, as I have been fully known."[1]

It feels as if these two scriptures were in conversation with each other, referring to each other. The Paul from 1 Corinthians 13 and the Paul from *The Acts of Paul and Thecla* feel connected here in Thecla's desire to be deemed worthy enough to stand face-to-face with him.

The expression "face-to-face" translates to me as "eye-to-eye," meaning on the same level, equal. The desire to be deemed worthy in order to stand face-to-face with love. The blueprints for constructing that unique bridge that will allow us to reclaim our sense of worth are invisible. Because each building site happens in the dark, from within. However, it's made visible here, in scripture from the first century about a young girl with no power outside her, building that bridge within her.

The hint to how Thecla managed to heal, how she found the worth that allowed her to imagine a new possibility for her life, is also right here in this first passage when we meet her. Her transformation begins by doing absolutely nothing. The scripture reads that Thecla "sat at a window," and "listened night and day," and that she "did not turn away from the window, but moved forward in faith." Thecla's spiritual transformation begins by her refusal to move, by her staying absolutely still. To the world around her, to her mother and fiancé, she is sitting at a window doing nothing. Internally, though, she is hard at work, allowing the stories she hears Paul share to awaken a latent knowing within her.

Maybe she recognized the essence of what Paul shared. Maybe she sensed the fruits of justice in his voice. Maybe all along she knew there had to be more, there had to be meaning, a river beneath the river, of the world she was born into. What's most significant here, though, is that the revolution from living a life that's expected of her to living the life she feels called to live begins with this, staying still. Staying still and just listening. Doing nothing externally, nothing that's normal, nothing that's habitual. She does nothing physically that's routine, that might perpetuate the life she had lived before. Instead, she stops. She sits still, and she begins listening intently. And she does not turn away. Thecla begins to transform her life by confronting all that surfaces from what she's hearing. She stays still, and she does not turn away from what images arise from shutting out the external world. She comes face-to-face with it all. With a rare form of courage we will be intimate with by the end of this book. A lion-hearted courage that's as treasured as a diamond, and as pressure-forged. The kind of courage that can't be seen, at least not at first.

At first, it just looks like refusing to continue on with life as is. It looks like sitting still, and refusing to participate in the life that even just yesterday still felt viable. It's a courage that allows us to want more for ourselves, more even than what our family and those who love us might want for us. It's a courage to begin the real and most valuable struggle of turning ourselves inside out. So that who we are in the innermost, truest place within us is who we are in the world around us. So that we begin to live from the relic in the shadow of our heart.

11.

The Body's Body

So Thamyris said to Theocleia, "Where is my Thecla?" And
Theocleia said, "I have a strange story to tell you. Indeed, for
three days and nights Thecla has not risen from the window—
either to eat or drink—but gazes as if looking upon some en-
joyable sight."

—*The Acts of Paul and Thecla* 8:2–4

The first time I saw Robert Lentz's icon of Mary
Magdalene, I was working at a Catholic charity program for pregnant teenagers in San Francisco. Mary
Magdalene had pride of place in a boardroom where the sisters
met to discuss each of the teens and their progress in the GED
program they offered them.

Mary Magdalene's official title according to the Catholic
Church since the sixth century was "the penitent prostitute."
More recently, in 2016, Pope Francis "rehabilitated" her title;
Mary Magdalene is now "the Apostle to the Apostles." Though,
to be clear, she is still not officially considered an apostle her-
self.

Mary Magdalene in Lentz's icon has a red muslin scarf

draped around her head and neck. Her skin is dark brown, and her name is written at the bottom center of the icon in Aramaic, one of the languages that scholars believe Christ spoke. She is holding up an egg in her left hand, and directing our attention to it with the pointer finger of her right hand.

Her eyes always stopped me in the hallway, and sort of commanded me to sneak into the empty boardroom to get a closer look. Her eyes are so insistent in the icon. Emphatic. They have secrets, and wisdom coiled into those radiant irises. And the love on her face, the fierce presence of it—I would just stand there and try to make sense of that much mystery.

My formal title was Childcare Counselor, and I found this curiously apt. I was hired to look after the babies and toddlers as the teens went to class with the sisters to earn their GEDs. But most of the time, the child I was really taking care of wasn't the infant but the infant's mom.

Something that deeply disturbed me was the constant reference or description of so many of the girls as "prostitutes." The median age of the majority of teens who came through this particular Catholic charity was fourteen. Some were sixteen or seventeen, and several were as young as eleven. But the majority of these new moms were just fourteen. My son's age now. They were children.

There was and is no other title to accurately describe them. And there is no such thing as a fourteen-year-old prostitute. There is only a child who has been left unprotected, without agency or true power.

These girls had been trafficked, and I can see that now. I can name it. But back then, in 2003, they were treated as if they had chosen prostitution as an occupation. And they were being shown mercy because they had chosen to keep their babies. They had chosen to take responsibility.

Choice. That's a very luxurious word and idea. This is something the girls taught me. Choice, personal agency, is the single most coveted luxury we can ever possess. Do we have a choice for the direction of our lives when the female body is still primarily treated as a commodity?

Cyntoia Brown was just sixteen years old when she was solicited at a Sonic Drive-In by forty-three-year-old real estate agent and youth pastor Johnny Allen in 2004. He offered her $150.

When Allen was found naked in bed, fatally shot with his own gun, Cyntoia was tried as an adult and sentenced to life in prison. During her trial, she never denied shooting Allen, but she said it was in self-defense.

While a runaway on the streets of Nashville, Cyntoia had met Garion McGlothen, known as Kut-Throat, who began trafficking her. According to Cyntoia, she was threatened, beaten, and sexually assaulted by Kut-Throat to force her to continue to support them financially.

In the groundswell of the #MeToo movement,[1] the injustice of Cyntoia Brown's case, and the multitude of other teenage girls tried as adults, was finally brought to light. Cyntoia Brown had served fifteen years of her life sentence when she was granted clemency on January 7, 2019.

During her incarceration, she had earned a GED, a liberal arts degree, and a bachelor's degree. She was referenced as a model prisoner at her clemency hearing before the Tennessee Board of Parole. Her name is now Cyntoia Brown Long, and unfortunately, her case is one among a multitude of cases where a girl or woman is imprisoned for protecting herself from sexual assault. A study of the California State Prison System revealed that close to 70 percent of the women imprisoned for murder had killed their partner while trying to protect themselves or their children. The first woman to be acquitted for using deadly force to protect herself from being raped was Joan Little in the mid-1970s. Little's case helped lay the initial groundwork for Battered Woman Syndrome, which is used as a defense or mitigating factor in cases involving self-defense from physical harm.[2]

The disparity between what was expected of the girls at the Catholic charity, what they were forced to face alone, compared to what was expected of the biological fathers of their children, weighed on me every day I worked as their childcare counselor. And the majority of the fathers were adults. Some were family members. Some were serving time. But all were exempt by law and cultural norms from radically changing their lives for the sake of the children they had fathered.

Most of the teens lived at the infant hospital because otherwise they would be unhoused, or seeking shelter in places that would endanger their lives and their newborns. Many had been kicked out of their homes for being pregnant. They were all angry, terrified, and traumatized.

A fight broke out one afternoon in the nursery, as I was demonstrating how to change a diaper without getting peed on in the process. Two teens had their chests puffed out, each threatening the other by posturing closer and closer until their very pregnant bellies were almost touching. I somehow managed to wedge myself between them. Then they proceeded to call each other every variation of the word "whore" I had ever heard; some were new to me.

And what hit me, what took a night of sobbing my face off to really take in, was that these two riotous moms were children. These two moms were children already entirely indoctrinated into this system of "purity" and "worth," of "guilt" and "shame," of valuing the virgin and terrorizing the whore.

For them, that word "whore" meant worthless. And nothing made me suffer more than experiencing firsthand, so firsthand I had spit on my face, how these invaluable girls felt absolutely without value in this world. When here they are giving birth to it. Here they are reconstituting the world's population with little to no power, and shame rather than praise or recognition.

Three, as I mentioned when introducing Paul, is the number of death and resurrection in the Christian story. Christ was crucified, and then on the third day was resurrected. Three, therefore, is an ancient number of transformation. It's also associated with the triple goddess: the maiden, mother, crone. A trinity that came long before Christianity's Trinity.

While seated at her window for three days and nights, Thecla transforms. She dies to the life she knew before. And what's "strange" about this for her mother, Theocleia, is that Thecla is no longer listening to her or to her fiancé, Thamyris.

I think this is why he asks, "Where is my Thecla?" As if Thecla is physically no longer there. She's no longer of "use" to him. She's disengaged with the economy of worth that would have her believe that she is what she can produce, she is what she can provide sexually, she is what she can give back to the family directly.

Thecla turns away from them, from how they want her to be, and turns inward instead. She's riveted in place, bound by the eternal kindness, the "sweetness" as the scripture earlier describes, of Paul's words about the beloved, Christ. She's entering a form of chrysalis.

For me, as a theologian, I interpret this pivotal three-day period of inner transformation as the critical next step after hearing the call. The next step is to remain still. Which can seem "strange" to a world that is constantly in motion, constantly impressed with the "hustle" and the "workaholic."

Staying still, not just for a moment but for "three days," is a chance to go deeper than otherwise possible. It's to listen to the body's body. It's to ask inwardly, who am I if I am not pleasing anyone? Who am I if I have no titles or names that signify my worth? And what is it that I truly want if I know I am already worthy just as I am?

Thecla listens inwardly, to what her own body has to say, rather than seeing her body as the world sees her, as a commodity. What's strange about this story for Thecla's mother, Theocleia, is that Thecla is opting out of this profoundly unjust system of associating her worth to her sex. She's choosing to die to what is expected of her simply because she's female. She's choosing a life that is not defined by what others want from her.

The fierce love I felt for these brave and traumatized young girls, these single moms, inspired me to enter my own kind of ministry. I entered seminary knowing I would never seek formal ordination. I would find the stories that included them, that spoke to them, that reached through to them. I would uncover the scripture that reminded them of the worth they were so convinced they had lost because of what had been done to their bodies.

I would find the ancient scripture that contains the story of a teenage girl who reclaims her choice in the world. And even more, I would find a way to suggest that it's the choice that makes anything sacred. It's having the choice to get married or not, to have children or not. It's the choice that's sacred. It's having that stillness, those proverbial three days, to hear what the body's body really wants. To get clear and free from the loud and pervasive expectation of marriage, of parenthood, and hear with an innate sense of self-worth what is really meant for us.

It's the reclamation of a choice for our own body that should be ours by the divine right of kings and queens, and protected by every court the world over, that should have always been ours, that should have fairy tales and children's books made about it. The choice at any point in our lives, no matter who we are, to be as strange as we need to be, to stay still longer than what's normal, to just stop and listen to what we actually want to say yes to. To do absolutely nothing for anyone else for as long as we need to, until we fully embody the answer we know is actually our own.

THE THIRD STAGE

A now visible door opens, and from somewhere mysterious, from this newfound possibility we didn't even know existed, courage rises up in us to walk through it. This is the third stage.

12

Courage

"And my daughter, like a spider in the window, also is bound to his words, held sway by new desire and fearful emotions. For the maiden fixates on the things he says and is captivated."

—*The Acts of Paul and Thecla* 9:2–3

There's a very rare form of courage that's too little understood or praised. It's not the kind of courage, for example, that looks the way Joan of Arc is most often portrayed—decked out in head-to-toe chain mail and taking on the Hundred Years' War like a medieval lady boss. It's not the external courage, the visible kind, the one we always focus on. It's the kind of courage it took for Joan to desire something new in her life, to desire a life that had never been lived before. It's the quiet, unseen moment, years before battle, when Joan said yes to the vision of a life that arrived from within her like an uninvited guest.

It takes a rare kind of courage to desire something new. Once we've heard the call, and reclaimed our inherent value in the world to know we're worthy of that calling, there's a quiet and uncelebrated bravery that comes from stepping toward a new possibility. This isn't about muscle and sweat, or sheer brawny physical power. This is about the origin of courage itself.

The word "courage" is derived from the Latin *cor*, meaning "heart." So Thecla's capacity to be "held sway by new desire," this is because of an inner strength, a unique form of courage that comes from within her. A courage that maybe Thecla's mother is jealous or afraid of, which is why she throws shade by calling her "a spider in the window."

Joan of Arc had no ambition to lead men into battle as a teenager. During her trial, when church authorities accused her of heresy, witchcraft, and violating divine law by dressing like a man, she said that she would have preferred to stay home spinning wool. But she was called from within to a life that had literally never happened before in her generation and in her part of the world. She was called to trust an inner voice that would guide her.

Of course, she displayed unprecedented bravery and loyalty to France through her actions, but what I want to magnify is that moment when Joan actually listened to the voice within her.

What happens when the objectified becomes the subject? What happens when the narrative changes, and the one who was meant to follow a predictable, predetermined, and well-worn path breaks new ground instead?

I want to illuminate the courage it takes to dare to feel a "new desire." We will soon witness in Thecla's story a series of brave external actions. But I want to draw a white chalk circle around this first, most courageous act that Thecla takes. It's real, and yet it can't be seen since it takes place from within her.

Thecla lets herself experience this new desire, which her mother describes as "fearful" emotions. Thamyris, her fiancé, the scripture reads, goes to Thecla's side both loving her and also fearing her passion. Why so much fear? Thecla is simply listening to Paul, and refusing to do anything other than that. She isn't harming anyone, or wielding a weapon—threatening their safety. She's simply listening to Paul's stories. In this setting, though, why is Thecla generating so much fear in those around her?

How I read this moment is that Thecla is displaying that silent, inner form of courage that allows her to shut out the external world and take her own heart seriously. She's listening foremost to what is happening from within because of what Paul is sharing. She is disengaging with the two most fundamental roles she is meant to fulfill, the roles of daughter and wife. And this generates fear because in this moment she is displaying the fact that she cannot be controlled. Thecla is simply demonstrating what has always been true: She has the capacity to free herself from their expectations. Thecla is realizing that she has all along been the subject of her own story, not an object in theirs.

Nigerian novelist and poet Chinua Achebe said in an interview, "Until the lions have their own historians, the history of the hunt will always glorify the hunter."[1] We don't know yet what Christianity looks like when we can all be seen as equals, no matter who we are, or who we love. We haven't heard yet fully what god is for the lion, only the hunter. I believe it's courage, the kind that comes from the heart, that forces the lion to refuse to move even when asked, or that lets the lion escape a cage the hunter created, even one built as if a home.

What do we call this form of inner courage? This quiet,

unassuming courage to finally start listening to that voice you may have been ignoring or discounting for most of your life?

To lionize the heart?

Supposedly the last words Joan of Arc said before she was burned at the stake were "Hold the cross so high that I may see it through the flames." In the decades to come, she would be exonerated of all charges and eventually made a saint. I still marvel, though, at the level of fear she generated by being someone who had never been before. For the crime of refusing to wear what was expected of her as a teenage girl. For refusing to be controlled, and refusing to be defined by the fact that she was female.

Maybe the real threat Joan posed was as living proof that the powerless can access endless possibilities, too. If we have the courage to act on the voice we hear within.

What does the lionized heart sound like?

It sounds like 156 young women standing up in the Ingham County courtroom and speaking directly to USA Gymnastics team doctor Larry Nassar about the impact his sexual assault had on them. It sounds like gymnast Aly Raisman when she said, "I am here to face you, Larry, so you can see I have regained my strength, that I am no longer a victim. I am a survivor."[2]

It sounds like fifteen-year-old Malala Yousafzai, when a member of the Taliban boarded a bus she was riding and waved a gun around at the terrified passengers to find the girl who had a death threat against her because she had dared to advocate for girls' education; and Malala said directly to his face, "I am Malala," right before he shot her in the head.

And then, years later, it sounds like the moment when Malala, after becoming the youngest Nobel Laureate, explains during her acceptance speech that, yes, "I am Malala," and also, "I am those 66 million girls who are deprived of education. . . . I am not raising my voice, it is the voice of those 66 million girls."[3]

It's the rare form of courage it takes to say something in a group that refuses to, in a group that remains silent and complicit to hate speech in any form. It's the courage it takes to claim the time we need to heal, to do the inner work that makes so much more possible. It's the courage it takes to choose to be single, instead of remaining with someone who provides comfort but causes pain. It's the courage it takes to express ourselves, to speak out, to come out, to dress, dance, and act in ways that no one else can compare us to. It's the courage it takes to believe in ourselves. It's the courage it takes to know something that's true about who we are, about what we want for our lives, so completely that we don't need anyone else to know it for us.

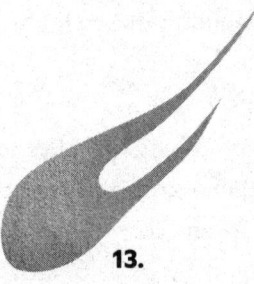

13.

Purpose

He said, "Thecla, my betrothed, why do you sit like this? What is the emotion that binds you in passion? Turn toward your Thamyris and be ashamed." And her mother also said the same things to her, "Child, why do you look down and sit like this, answering nothing but acting like a mad person?" And they cried desperately—Thamyris for the loss of his wife, Theocleia for the loss of her child.... So there was great confusion and mourning in the house. And while these things were happening, Thecla did not turn back, but was fixed to the word of Paul.

—*The Acts of Paul and Thecla* 10:1–6

In *The Gospel of Mary,* there's this moving scene; I see it vividly as if a scene from a film every time I read it. Christ's disciples are terrified after his crucifixion. Understandably, they fear that if Christ was killed by the Roman Empire, they'll be next. They feel bereft, disoriented.

"Then Mary stood up," her gospel says (5:4).[1] She tenderly kisses them and refers to them as her brothers and sisters. She comforts them. She becomes a presence of love when love is most needed. She reminds them, "Do not weep, do not be distressed nor be in doubt. For his grace will be with you sheltering you. Rather praise his greatness, for he has united us and made us true Human beings" (5:5–8).[2]

As I mentioned in the chapter "Purity," the Greek word translated as "true Human beings" is *anthropos*. From the Greek more directly, *anthropos* refers to the state of what it means to be human; it refers to the human condition of being both a mortal, egoic self, and also an eternal soul. Both, simultaneously.

This human condition, no matter what we do for a living—this being both fully human and fully divine—this is our purpose. Our purpose—which Christ reminded Mary and the disciples they were to live out, and that Mary in her gospel, in his absence, reminded the disciples they were to continue to practice—is to be a self that merges with the soul.

After Mary said these reassuring words to the disciples, her gospel relates that "she turned their mind toward the Good" (5:9).[3] "The Good" is how her gospel refers to god. So Mary turned their "mind," or the Greek *nous,* meaning the spiritual eye of the heart, back from the ego, and all of its captivating seven powers, toward god, toward the Good. Mary here through her example turns the disciples away from fear and division back to a sense of unity, of becoming the love they can perceive from within.

Purpose here is not based on what we do to support ourselves and our family—not primarily, at least. That's a job, a career, or a calling, a vocation. Purpose here relates to the actual nature of who we are, to how we are living out this remembrance of being fully human and fully divine. This is a universal condition, of being both a messy egoic human self and a soul of love. That is our purpose. To try and fail and try again to love and be loved, to grow that capacity, that forgotten organ of sight in the heart, that allows us to see and know love. So that we can also recognize then all that is not love, and all that is not meant for us.

In 1986, a year before his death, at a lecture in Amherst on the responsibility and role of the writer in society, James Baldwin said, "The reason that Plato wanted no poets in his republic is because a writer is, by definition, a disturber of the peace."

The reason I was never confused in divinity school and seminary that I would ever become a minister is that I knew without yet having the confidence to claim it that I was studying to become a theologian so that I could write. So that I could write about god. So that I could disturb and disrupt our ideas about god. So that I could articulate in new ways very ancient ideas about god; and about what it means to be human.

The greatest challenge I had in becoming a writer was the judgment that writing was in a way doing nothing, or not doing enough. I felt more "purposeful" being in direct service to others, especially working with children. It made me feel as though my contribution was real, visibly concrete. And I was praised for the work I did, but for me personally, I never felt that sense of praise inwardly. I felt like I was hiding. And if I ever mentioned my writing, I talked about it with this horrible mix of shame, feeling both selfish and inadequate.

When I write a sentence that says something real to me, I feel a sense of accomplishment I can't even explain. Like hearing a sudden gospel choir within me, I feel this immediate and immeasurable praise. No external or financial compensation compares to it. It's this inner state of knowing I am doing exactly what I'm meant to.

In order to become a writer, it meant working as a childcare counselor and then a meditation teacher to support myself and later my son, but slowly starting to identify as a writer, saying it out loud even, creating space for it no matter how hard it was to justify the time it took to do it. And no matter who I might disappoint in the process. Saying no to holidays and vacations and staying in my various small apartments over the years to write instead. Saying no to people and events that distract and derail me from hearing the still, small voice that I can meet with here in this silence writing creates. The voice that is a personal experience of true power, because its presence overwhelms the self-doubt that tries to silence me from within.

It's a voice that asks me to find a way to stand up like Mary in my own life when others question the purpose of my work or when I'm in disbelief that I'll ever figure out a way to siphon what feels like an ocean inside me. Writing asks me to practice this ultimate purpose of being fully human, of becoming a presence of comfort and belief to those places in me that before were filled with judgment and dread.

Thamyris and Theocleia, Thecla's fiancé and mother, are mourning the "loss" of her. Thecla is no longer in relation to their needs or their expectations of her. She's relating only to what her soul desires, "the word of Paul." In truth, of course, they haven't "lost" her. Thecla is sitting right there in front of them. She hasn't moved. But inwardly, she has gone to where they can't follow.

Thamyris suggests Thecla should turn toward him and "be ashamed." That she should feel shame for having the courage to be who she is, rather than being who he needs her to be. Thecla's mother calls her "a mad person," which all just feels so familiar to me, and really to any one of us who tries to do what we feel called to do versus what our family, friends, or community might expect us to. We're called crazy. Crazy for wanting more, or not even more—just for wanting what's meant for us. What we're meant to do, that singular thing that forces us to forgive and love ourselves fiercely in order to do it.

And then they both cry, desperately, for losing what they felt was owed them—for Thamyris a wife, and for Theocleia a daughter. Thecla is right there, seated in front of them. But she's existing now outside of the conditions they had set for loving her, for being in their lives. Thecla is fixated now, riveted by the words of Paul. She has stepped outside of the conditional love she had known before and has entered the realm of what's unconditional. The love she's related to now doesn't come from outside of her. It is there in the stillness. It is there where Paul's words are finding her from within.

Professor and author Brené Brown writes, "I am here for my purpose. I'm not here to make people comfortable or to be liked. My purpose is to know and experience love. This means excavating the unsaid. In the world and in me."[4] After we find the courage to listen to what we hear within, to lionize the heart, in order to begin to take action on what we hear, it's important to understand that our purpose is who we are, not what we do for a living. Our purpose is to love and be loved, to find what asks us to expand our capacity to know love.

When I sit to write, I am most often just sitting here, seemingly doing nothing. And this sitting still is what I judged as not enough because externally it's marked by a profound lack of obvious productivity. My internalized Theocleia screamed "crazy lady" at me for so many years. But in my time "doing nothing," I've been "excavating the unsaid" as Brown directs. I've been using sentences like drawbridges to enter places within myself previously inaccessible. I've been quietly assigning value to what's intangible and yet also invaluable. I've been weaving together with words sentences that work like elixirs, as if words could heal from the reading alone.

We are not here to live out someone else's expectation of us; to fit into the conditions someone else has set for us in order to be loved. Our purpose is to know love, from the Greek *gnosis,* meaning knowledge gained from direct experience. We are here to know and experience love directly. And this is what makes turning inward so critical. Because we can never truly be loved if we aren't also revealing and articulating the truth of who we are. Our purpose is to love ourselves enough to be authentic, integral. And this means disentangling from all those lures cast in our direction from people and positions of power that might suggest we will be loved if . . . or then. Our purpose is to confront the voices within and around us that suggest love is conditional. Our purpose is to stand up amidst the doubt, the name-calling, the shame-throwing, and become a presence of love even in the absence of it.

THE FOURTH STAGE

Then there's the inevitable pilgrimage that this new way of seeing demands, compels us to take. And this pilgrimage, this adventure, inexorably forces us to unravel the old way of understanding ourselves and what's possible. This pilgrimage tests us to see if we're really ready to let go of how we used to operate in the world, of who we used to be. This is the fourth stage.

If we can survive the tests of the fourth stage, which tend to be both mental and physical and bring us to a point of choosing—of counting our losses and returning to what we had, to who we used to be, to how we used to live, even if we know how limited it is now, how small, even if we've tasted something more infinite—we're often given a chance to go back to what we know. To play it safe. To return to the traps and cages we once called home.

14.

Possession

Rising early in the morning, [Thamyris] went to the house of
Onesiphorus with the rulers, public officials, and a large crowd
with clubs, saying to Paul, "You have corrupted the city of the
Iconians and also my betrothed so that she will not want me.
Let us go to the governor Castellius." And the whole crowd
said, "Arrest the magician! For he has corrupted all of our
wives and has seduced the masses!"

—*The Acts of Paul and Thecla* 15:1–2

Demas and Hermogenes come back into the story.
They were the ones in chapter four who compelled
Onesiphorus to invite them into his house to hear
Paul preach, even though "the fruits of justice" weren't visible
in their faces. Thamyris invites them over in order to ply them
with drinks in the hopes they'll spill the beans about what Paul
said or did that made Thecla turn from him. They suggest that
Thamyris bring Paul to the governor on the charge of "seduc-
ing the masses to the new teaching of the Christians," because
then, they reason, "he will kill him, and you will have your wife
Thecla" (14:1).[1] And the scripture reads that when Thamyris

heard what Demas and Hermogenes said, "he was filled with jealousy and wrath" (15:1).[2]

According to *The Gospel of Mary,* the seventh power is the power of wrath. This is an egoic state of rage that makes us feel that we're justified in expressing our anger and can take action on it. In my research of the seven powers in *The Gospel of Mary,* I've always wondered if wrath is the seventh because it is the most derailing, gripping, and intoxicating of all the powers. Maybe it's the seventh because it's the most difficult to snap out of, and the most blinding. When we see this moment through the lens of powers listed in *The Gospel of Mary,* we know that Thamyris is currently drunk on his own ego. And I can infer from this reference to the powers of wrath and jealousy in *The Acts of Paul and Thecla* that the two scriptures might be in conversation with each other. Meaning the one is made more comprehensible by knowing the other.

The modern-day list of the seven deadly sins includes both of the words used to describe Thamyris: wrath and envy, or jealousy. The traditional deadly sins are Lust, Gluttony, Greed, Sloth, Wrath, Envy, and Pride. What's fascinating is that these sins are not listed together in the New Testament. The history of their formation is rooted in Egypt with a fourth-century monk named Evagrius. His list included an eighth, the sin of sadness: Gluttony, Prostitution, Greed, Sadness, Wrath, Dejection, Boasting, and Pride. Christian monk and theologian John Cassian translated Evagrius's list for the Latin-speaking West as: "Gluttony, Lust, Greed, Despair, Wrath, Sloth, Vainglory, and Pride." By 590 C.E., Pope Gregory revised the list down to seven deadly sins by melding Despair into Sloth, and Vainglory into Pride, and then he added Envy.

In one of his spiritual works, titled *The Institutes of the Coenobia,* Cassian gives instructions for cenobitic monasticism in

Egypt, which began in the early fourth century. Cenobitic monasticism refers to a monastic tradition that stresses communal life, whereas eremitic monasticism refers to a hermit's life of unbroken solitude. So Cassian's *Institutes* were written essentially to instruct monks on how to live together in a way that elevates their spiritual lives and limits the amount of inevitable drama that close quarters breed. Books five to twelve of Cassian's *Institutes* address the original eight sins or vices and how to cure them.

The three stages to the mystical path of the Egyptian desert ascetics were *Purgatio, Illuminatio,* and *Unitio.* The vices or sins were a part of the *Purgatio* stage, or in Greek, *Catharsis.* This is the critical stage when the monks become aware of their egoic desires and learn how to manage them.[3] The answer for Cassian was not only to become aware of those desires but also to remove the aspects of life that might tempt or rile up the powers as well. Hence, celibacy. Periodic starvation. High walls around the monastery. A sealed-off existence.

Once the first stage is mastered, the monk moves into *Illuminatio,* or in Greek, *Theoria.* With the heart clear of the egoic powers, the direct teachings of Christ can be received, revealed through meditation. (This is the spiritual process described in *The Gospel of Mary.*) And finally, the monk can enter *Unitio,* or in Greek, *Theosis.* This is the stage of mystical union with Christ. It's to achieve a state of being in constant dialogue with the voice of love from within. Most monks never reached this stage, and remained in a dance between the first and second stages.

What's so profoundly curious to me is the glaring absence of any reference to the earlier roots of the seven deadly sins within *The Gospel of Mary* as originally the seven powers. Powers of the ego, not sins. And powers that Christ gave to a woman long before women were excluded from the practice itself of reaching *Unitio* within the church. The three fragments that have been found of *The Gospel of Mary* were not recovered at Nag Hammadi, but rather were each discovered individually, one at an antiquities market in Cairo, and two along the Nile in Egypt. There is no empirical evidence to suggest that John Cassian read *The Gospel of Mary* while he was in Egypt.

However, in the early fifth century, Cassian returned from Egypt and traveled to an area in France that is known as La Sainte Baume, "The Sacred Mountain" or "The Holy Balm." It's a mountain ridge that extends between the regions of Bouches-du-Rhône and Var in southern France. This is where legends say that Mary Magdalene lived out the remaining years of her life after escaping Roman persecution by crossing the Mediterranean Sea to the South of France and then heading north to hide in the caves of Sainte Baume. In the early fifth century, Cassian established a priory there in her honor, and his feast day according to the Roman Catholic Church is the day after Mary Magdalene's; hers is on July 22, and his is on July 23.

Blinded with wrath and jealousy, Thamyris wakes up early the next day after his drinks night with Demas and Hermogenes and charges over to Onesiphorus's house with, as the scripture relates, "the rulers, the public officials, and a large crowd with clubs saying to Paul, 'You have corrupted the city of Iconium and also my betrothed so that she will not want me'" (15:1).[4]

The word "possession" comes from the Latin *possessus,* which means "to have and hold, hold in one's control, to be the master of, to own." Thamyris is gripped by the misunderstanding that a human being, any human being, has the right to possess another. And he feels entitled to that right of possessing Thecla because of love. Thamyris believes that it's his love for Thecla that gives him the right to "have her for his wife." And his love for her also gives him the right to stir up an angry mob in order to destroy the life she has chosen instead of him.

Love, though, has nothing to do with possession, with treating other human beings as if they exist for us, as if they are ours "to have and to hold." Love is not ownership. Love is the opposite of control. Thamyris acts from his wrathful egoic state, thinking he is justified to reclaim Thecla, who was actually never his to begin with. Love does not justify acting as if we could ever possess someone. Only the ego does that. And so here we arrive at the missed opportunity. And here we can learn from the fatal mistake that Thamyris makes. He mistakes his wrath and jealousy as evidence of his love, when these egoic states are not yet love at all.

He calls in the governor, the officials, the angry mob that will soon light the fire on Thecla's pyre, which sets the wheels in motion for the trials Thecla will have to face in order for her transformation to be complete. Thamyris could have moved past the *Purgatio*, the *Catharsis*, and entered into a more illuminated existence where real love begins to become clear, where loving Thecla would mean letting her go. Or where loving Thecla would mean understanding that he never had a claim on her soul from the start. And that this teacher Paul who is in her life is not in competition with him for "ownership" of her. Paul is reminding Thecla of the freedom that has always existed within her. The freedom to shed every role society placed on her, and to find what's actually true for her.

Even if at a great cost. Instead, Thamyris joins the crowd, his voice blending into the chant from the angry mob, "Arrest the magician!"

It's not magic, of course, that Paul wields. It's love. And that's the real threat; that's what conjures the wrath and the jealousy and the fear the mob embodies. Because real love liberates.

15.

Love

And Paul lifted up his voice, saying...."In that one, humans have hope, who alone had compassion for a wandering world so that humanity might no longer be under judgment, but have trust and fear of God, and knowledge of dignity and a love of truth."

—*The Acts of Paul and Thecla* 17:1–2

First there's the love that most of us have known, the love that seeks to have and to hold. The love that limits because it is limited. The love that's rooted in the ego. The love that wants us to change and then to remain exactly the same. The love that has ultimatums and conditions. The love that the ego uses to try to find outside of us what can actually only be found within. It's a very reasonable love; it's a love that loves within the lines. It's a bounded love that only goes where love has been before.

Then there's a love that liberates.

The love that most of us long for is out beyond conditions. It's a love that's limitless because its source is without end. It's a love that is sourced from inside us. It's a love that's rooted in the soul. It's an unreasonable love. It rarely loves within the lines. It breaks the rules, loves wildly, loudly, will march through the streets if it has to, will hold hands with anyone who is suffering, even a perceived enemy.

And the love that liberates changes us rather than asks what it loves to change. Because it's a love that reaches what has never been loved before. It's a love that reaches to where we are most human, where we feel dead and broken, where we feel caged and unfree, and it frees us with its presence.

And this is the love most of us long for, because we know in our heart's heart that it's all that matters. What matters in this brief time we have here is giving all of our love away— knowing as we do that this source of love is limitless, is within us, and is also more than we could ever be separate from it. All that matters is this actual treasure, which we only possess by giving away. This longed-for love is found in these moments when we can give up the small egoic self for the sake of someone else, for the sake of becoming a part of something that is beyond us.

The concept of marriage predates the world religions. Earliest records of its existence begin around 2350 B.C.E. Marriage was primarily a form of trade, where the bride was the bargaining chip, a strategic form of human barter used between two families to create generational wealth or to establish a truce between feuding families. It was a transactional exchange, a binding contract. So marriage did not begin within any one religion, and marriage did not begin with love.

Within the history of Christianity, the concept of marriage as a sacrament (and the requirement then for a priest's blessing) wasn't a widely accepted ceremony until the eighth century. It was formally written into canon law at the Council of Trent in 1563. In Thecla's lifetime, girls were most often married as teenagers to much older men. A girl, once she became a wife, was the property of her husband. She was entirely at the mercy of his temperament. He had the right by Roman law to punish her in any way he saw fit, including killing her. When a girl became a bride, she became property that could never own property herself.

Let's get Old Testament for a moment.

The word "torah" in Hebrew means to "instruct," or "teach." The Torah is a compilation of the first five books of the Old Testament; these books are Genesis, Exodus, Leviticus, Numbers, and Deuteronomy. The established timeframe for when scholars estimate the scripture in the Old Testament was written spans between 1450 B.C.E. and 430 B.C.E. The origins of three world religions are woven together with these same five books as their most ancient monotheistic scripture: Judaism, Christianity, and Islam.

From Genesis 2:18–23: "The Lord God said, 'It is not good for the man to be alone. I will make a helper suitable for him.' . . . The man said, 'This is now bone of my bones and flesh of my flesh; she shall be called "woman," for she was taken out of man'" (NIV). I'll be the first to admit that the man has some seriously seductive sway with that "bone of my bones, flesh of my flesh" line. It gets me every time. It's just when the man explains why he named his helpmeet "woman" that my eyes clear up and my focus returns: "for she was taken out of man." I would laugh long and hard if this wasn't so much at the root of how the subjugation of women has been justified within the Abrahamic traditions of Judaism, Christianity, and Islam for millennia.

The man here has taken a power that is exclusively reserved for those who have a womb—the power of making a body within the body—and has made it his own.

If we ever needed proof for the origin story of religion's control over the female body, it's here. In this reality-defying feat of assuming a power that is actually female, and then telling us that we're in fact made the weaker for it.

The man here is not unlike the magician, a skilled illusionist who creates a great distraction so that we're mesmerized by the smoke that's suddenly wafting all around us—the illusion that menstruation is unholy, that the female body has the power to defile, that childbirth is a punishment for Eve's audacious apple eating, for daring to want to *know* truth in her own body. We soon forget to look at the true source of his magic right here between our own legs.

I love weddings. My own was one of the best days of my life. I wore a red dress, of course. I'm especially moved when I watch those unions that can happen now but were illegal not so long ago, like Mildred and Richard Loving, who were sentenced to a year in prison in Virginia for their interracial relationship. They appealed their conviction, which ended in the legalization of interracial marriage in the 1967 Supreme Court case *Loving v. Virginia*. Mildred Loving left us with these words: "I believe all Americans, no matter their race, no matter their sex, no matter their sexual orientation, should have the same freedom to marry."[1]

Legally recognized same-sex marriages only recently included all fifty states within the U.S., thanks to the Supreme Court case *Obergefell v. Hodges* in 2015. A subsequent nationwide study conducted at Johns Hopkins University found that the establishment of same-sex marriage directly impacted the rate of teenage suicide. Approximately 134,000 fewer teens committed suicide each year after it became a possibility for them to marry someone no matter their sex or gender.[2] Marriage has come a long way and a lot closer to actually being about love. However, child marriages remain legal in forty-two states, and according to the United Nations, approximately twelve million girls globally are forced to marry each year.[3]

There's an issue with marriage that only becomes visible once Thecla refuses to participate in it. Because there were no laws or societal rules that protected her or provided her with a choice.

What happens when we untangle our sense of self-worth from these expected roles we're conditioned to fulfill as partners? What happens when love is what we are, not what we earn or have to prove we're worthy of? What happens when meeting someone just adds to the love that's already sourced from within?

I remember the moment I found out in a women's history course in college that a woman couldn't open a bank account on her own without a signature from her husband until 1974, when the Equal Credit Opportunity Act passed. So more than half the population has only had full control of how they spend and invest their money for the last fifty years. This feels like a tangible vestige of what Thecla refused to participate in, the collusion of love and ownership. The unholy mixing of love and control.

I had a text-thread conversation recently with a close writer friend who also perpetually finds herself unattached. And she reminded me of something that's easy to forget—that up until just this past century, a woman had no other place in society except to be married. This could explain why currently there's a record-breaking number of unmarried women in the U.S.[4] We're single maybe just because we can be.

I never dreamt of my wedding day as a little girl. I dreamt of a less traditional arrangement, like the conjoined houses of the Mexican painters Frida Kahlo and Diego Rivera—connected by a bridge between them. There's this scene in the film *Frida,* with Salma Hayek, that I recognized as the truest truth for me when it comes to love. Whether I ever got married, it's what I wanted most for myself, and now, if I ever marry again, it's what I want to remain. Frida asks her father what she wanted to be when she was a little girl, and her father responds, "You wanted to be your own person."

I was ambivalent about marriage, but I was unequivocal about wanting two things: a great love story—to know love, to experience it directly—and to have a baby. That desire, motherhood, was almost otherworldly. What I mean is that it felt as if I missed my son before he was born. It was as if the love I had for him was waiting, unspent within me until I finally got the chance to share it with him. It felt heavy at times, oppressive even, because I wasn't in control of when or if I would finally look him in the face, hold him in my arms. I couldn't listen to the song "To Zion" by Lauryn Hill without bawling—especially the bit when she describes how much it is just to wait outside her son's bedroom door, how she's never felt a love like this before. By my early thirties, I had experienced several loving, long-term relationships, but each had ended once marriage came up. Because I didn't feel ready, or that it was right. Or maybe it's that I wasn't certain if I felt "in love, in love." Until the day I met my son's dad.

We were in a grocery store, of all places. And when our eyes met, my skin started to vibrate imperceptibly like a tuning fork. I wasn't just attracted to him; my eyes felt caught. As if our gaze, our sightline, was actual filament from a fishing rod that got tangled. And we couldn't figure out how to untie the knot before unintentionally staring for too long as we passed each other, long enough that we had to turn our heads because our tangled sight of each other wouldn't let us look away.

Several days later, I was standing in line at the cafeteria of the school where I taught World Religions to seventh graders after seminary. Suddenly, my skin went off again like a gong, vibrating as if detecting an inaudible sound, a unique pitch his presence cast in my direction. So I turned my head. And sure enough, my son's dad was there at the end of the same line I was in. We worked at the same school down the street from the grocery store where we met.

As a kid, I had a pet snapping turtle named Herman, for a brief period until he clamped onto my brother's pointer finger so successfully that even as he whipped back his finger in alarm, there was Herman holding tight, entirely unfazed, a complete bastion of the refusal to let go.

I was Herman when it came to the man I married; I couldn't let go. It was the most obstinate and unyielding love I've ever known. It refused to give up. As if everything that was meant for me was on the other side of figuring out how to become a love he didn't want to leave. Even after he divorced me, even after we went through several post-divorce reconciliations, even after it continued to end in the same way, and with a heartbreak that hollowed me out each time.

To my shock, my eventual shame, and to my wide-eyed awareness that choosing him meant being alone again, I still felt this compulsion to say yes when he wanted to give it one more try. Just in case, this time . . .

I felt shame because after years of trying, saying yes began to mean betraying that quiet voice of knowing inside me. Choosing him began to mean abandoning myself. And shame because Strong Independent Woman was my primary identity.

Yet here I was with my jaw clamped shut for over a decade on a marriage that had barely lasted a year. Here I was being yanked and throttled by a love that kept breaking me, and yet, despite my independence, I felt powerless to let go. Some call this bond trauma, others karma. For me, I call this being neck-deep in the second power from *The Gospel of Mary,* the power of desire. Or "Clinging," which is how I renamed it—but we'll get to that in chapter seventeen, "Death."

I used to have this recurring dream that I was locked in the attic and only he had the key. Love felt like that to me. That I had somehow given him the power to hold me captive. He had all the control to just come visit when he felt like it. And to stay for only as long as he wanted. In the dream, the hardest part wasn't that he locked me in when he left. It was that I would just sit there each time he did. I would just sit there and wait. As if living on rations was all that was meant for me.

After Thamyris has Paul arrested, he stands before the court "crying out loudly," and says, "Proconsul, this person—we do not know where he is from—who does not allow maidens to marry, let him say to you on what account he teaches these things" (16:1).[5]

And Paul responds by talking about god. Or about his understanding of god. He explains to the governor, and to the entire proconsul that has gathered there in the wake of Thecla's refusal to move from her windowsill, her refusal to marry: "In that one, humans have hope, who alone had compassion for a wandering world so that humanity might no longer be under judgment, but have trust and fear of God, and knowledge of dignity and a love of truth" (17:2).[6]

Paul argues in the end that he only teaches what is revealed to him, so what wrong or harm could he possibly cause? But the governor is not impressed, and orders for Paul to be bound and carried off to prison.

Maybe the wrong or harm Paul has caused this small town in ancient Turkey is the inevitable outcome of what happens when love is untangled from the patriarchal threads in marriage, when a more ultimate source of love is revealed, a love more binding than any earthly contract.

Canadian poet and novelist Margaret Atwood says, "The desire to be loved is the last illusion: give it up and you will be free."[7] Maybe this is what was so threatening about Thecla's refusal to marry. It's this undercurrent, this subtext that says, I am free. I am free because I've given up the illusion that I need to be loved (by someone outside of me). I am free because I am my own. I know that love is ultimately sourced from within me. So marriage, then, when and if it comes, arrives as a choice, and as an addition to an already abundant existence of love.

Maybe what Thecla heard wasn't exactly what Paul said. Maybe when Paul taught about god, about the hope and compassion offered to this "wandering world," what Thecla heard was something like this:

You don't have to be loved to receive it. You don't have to do anything, prove anything. You don't have to become what someone else needs you to be. You don't have to follow the rules and expectations of a society that sees you as a commodity, a transaction. You don't have to perform, audition for someone's love for you. Love is what you inherit as you open your eyes. Love is what waits for you when you can return to a place softer than fear or hatred. Love is what is here for you from within you. Love is not what you go out to search for.

Love is what waits for you to return to it. Here in this body we too often abandon, too often overlook. Here in this body that we're never told is the holy of holies. Love waits for us to realize it, sees out through our eyes. Love waits for us to return to it. Finally. After all our searching ends. Love is here within.

16.

Nakedness

But in the night Thecla took off her bracelets and gave them
to the gatekeeper, and the door was opened for her. She went
into the prison and gave the jailer a silver mirror. She went in
to Paul and sat at his feet, and she heard the great things of
God. And Paul feared nothing having rights in the freedom of
God, and Thecla strengthened her trust, kissing his chains.

—*The Acts of Paul and Thecla* 18:1–2

Love undresses the ego.

When the scripture last mentions Thecla, before
we find her here in chapter eighteen visiting the
prison in order to see Paul, her mother and fiancé are begging
her to come away from the window—calling her "a mad-
woman" and telling her she should be ashamed—but "Thecla
did not turn back" (10:6).[1] She did not turn back. And this is
critical. If we want to live into what might be next, what we
truly desire for our lives, we can't turn back to the old one.

The life that was expected of Thecla tried to pull her back
into it through the mental anguish of guilt and shame, of feeling as though she were directly harming her mother and fiancé

by choosing a new life for herself. Thecla's mother asks her, "Child, why do you look down and sit like this, answering nothing?" (10:4). For me, Thecla is looking down because she is drawn inward.

She's "answering nothing," I think, because right now she's on an unseen, and too often unrecognized, form of pilgrimage—not one made in miles and distance. It's an internal depth. This is about that unexplored territory most of us are terrified of—it's about existing intensely within ourselves for long enough to actually see who we are. So, it's not just about staying still; it's also about staying present. It's an inner quest. The word "quest" comes from the Old French *quester,* based on the Latin *quaerere,* meaning "to ask or seek." Thecla refuses to answer these questions her mother and fiancé demand of her because their questions are no longer her own. She's not responsible for their confusion. She's committed now to asking herself the most fundamental question we can ever live into: Who am I?

And she's intentionally looking down, I think, because she's disengaging with the life that she has turned away from. She's ceasing to exist solely for others; she's demanding that she exist most importantly within herself. She's tending to that sapling, that tiny green shoot that has begun to grow within her. A sense of self-worth. A sense of dignity. A lion-hearted courage to live more ardently, more authentically. A tendril of pride. A knowing of how needed her one voice is in this movement that has formed in the wake of Christ. For me, this is such a clear demonstration of the power of meditation. This is an example of meditation as an act of resistance.

"Thecla did not turn back." She refuses to let their verbal hooks land and be reeled back into the life she was born into. She remains within. She allows their words to fall all around her. She refuses to make eye contact with her old life so that she can remain focused on the vision of what might come next. Then in the night, Thecla ends her three-day vigil by visiting the prison where Paul is being held.

The scripture reads that Thecla took off her bracelets and gave them to the gatekeeper, "and the door was opened to her" (18:1).[2] If we read the text both literally and metaphorically, we can imagine that she had to pay a price, or a bribe to the guard, in order for him to let her into the prison. We can also imagine that the bracelets might represent the trappings, or the glittery chains of her gender, that to be born a girl in her world meant to dress as one, meant she was adorned as one not necessarily to please herself but as an object to please others. She takes off her bracelets, her egoic identity as a girl, as a possession, as a gender that is considered "less than" within the Roman Empire, as a person that is not whole in herself. Thecla takes off all that her bracelets might mean, and proceeds deeper into the prison toward Paul.

Next, Thecla faces the jailer. And to gain entrance, she gives him "a silver mirror." The mirror, of course, only reflects our external image. We can only see the self that the world sees in a mirror. We can't see what's within us reflected in it. It's just the surface, just a reflection of the self we present to the world. So Thecla hands over her silver mirror as payment to the jailer to be with Paul in his prison cell. She surrenders the egoic self, the girl she let the world believe she was, in order to face Paul as she really is.

This moment in Thecla's story reminds me again of Paul's first letter to the Corinthians, when he says, "As yet we see, in a mirror, dimly, but then—face-to-face! As yet my knowledge is incomplete, but then I will know in full, as I have been fully known."[3] Thecla discards the mirror as if the mirror is and has

always been an intermediary, a vision once removed, an allur-
ing yet ultimately indirect source of knowledge. She turns
away from the reflection of her face, of how she has been presenting herself externally to the world, and she chooses instead
to meet face-to-face with the experience of love itself.

This is a pivotal moment in her story, and it's only possible
because "Thecla did not turn back." She takes off her bracelets
and gives away her silver mirror. She gives away the objects
that identified her as an object, the possessions that marked
her as a possession. She moves, paradoxically, deeper into the
prison, and closer to a freedom she has never known before.
She sits beside Paul and hears "the great things of God"
(18:1).[4] And she strengthens her trust in this new life she had
chosen, "kissing his chains" (18:2).

The spiritual motif of nakedness runs throughout the world
religions. In the ancient Sumerian version of the goddess Inanna's descent into the underworld, which could date as early as
4000 B.C.E., she discards an article of clothing or jewelry at
each of the seven gates in order to continue to descend further.
And when Inanna finally reaches the underworld, to reunite
with her lost sister, or symbolically a lost source of her true
power, she's fully naked.

There's a rebellion in nakedness. There's a power in no
longer hiding. There's a nearness to what's divine that we can
only reach by discarding the "clothes" we wear at times to
make other people comfortable, or to demonstrate our own
conformity. I'm speaking metaphorically here, but the literal
can reclaim power, too. From seventeenth-century Quaker
women in the Massachusetts Bay Colony walking naked in
public to protest against orthodox Puritans, to the modern-
day feminist group Femen, who protest topless to demand

women's rights—if we become uncontrollable, the oppressive currency of purity can be used to liberate.

In September 2022, a twenty-two-year-old Iranian woman, Mahsa Amini, was beaten to death in Tehran by the Guidance Patrol for allegedly not wearing the hijab appropriately, allowing some of her hair to fall down past her head covering. I remember, viscerally, seeing the first videos of women burning their hijabs and cutting their hair as a response to Amini's murder. I felt a rage that unified me with them, that surged through me and transported me, as if I were standing with them around the bonfire they had lit.

Within weeks, social media was flooded with videos of women from around the world showing their solidarity by cutting their hair and burning clothes that enforce gender norms. A global awareness became crystalline about the vast and pervasive ways women's bodies are controlled. It isn't the headscarf that's inherently oppressive; as feminist scholar Leila Ahmed articulates in "The Discourse of the Veil," some Muslim women find it freeing, and a revered way to express their faith. It's the lack of choice that creates the oppression. It's this stolen right to define our self, to dress true to that self, and to self-identify.

I don't know the inside of that kind of courage, but I recognize it, and I revere it. I don't know that level of bravery. But I know what it means to have choices taken from me because I'm female. I know what it means to think carefully about when I go out, and where, and never alone at night. I know what it means to be told and taught that I am responsible for my own safety, that if I don't want to draw too much attention, or be blamed for an assault, I must behave like this, and dress like this, and be nice like this, and present to the world a woman who isn't too attractive, or threatening, or sexy, or too intelligent that she makes a man feel inadequate. I know what it's like to live in a world that demands I wear the outer garments of a "good girl."

There's a dialogue in *The Gospel of Mary* between the second power, desire, which is the clinging type of desire that comes from the ego. This egoic desire says, "I did not see you go down, yet now I see you go up. So why do you lie since you belong to me?" And the soul answers, "I saw you. You did not see me nor did you know me. You mistook the garment I wore for my true self. And you did not recognize me" (9:1–4).[5] The soul wears "garments" or layers of the egoic self. This is needed, and sometimes lifesaving. We aren't always safe to reveal all that we are.

Yet, the practice that's being illuminated here is to know, as in, to experience directly the truth of our identity, which is not rooted in these egoic layers but in the soul. "You mistook the garment I wore for my true self. And you did not recognize me."

The spiritual practice of the ancient Christ Movement aimed to do just this, to remember that the true self is the soul not the ego. This is the path I mentioned in the chapter "Purity," the kenotic path. *Kenosis* comes from the Greek verb *kenosein,* which means "to empty oneself." So the kenotic path means we empty, or release, or strip off the self we are wearing, the egoic self that we may have been over-identifying with for some time, and reveal the soul of love that remains underneath. Cynthia Bourgeault, in *The Meaning of Mary Magdalene,* explains: "Stripping oneself and standing naked: this is the essence of the kenotic path."[6]

Love undresses the ego.

Healing for me has always looked like a chambered nauti-lus. As if each next time I heal, I am nearing closer and closer to the thing itself, spiraling further inward to where the actual wound was first made, where it waits for me to return to it. As if I have to first accrue the amount of love that can actually heal it; I have to become a love that can reach it.

We were in what would be our last therapy session together. We had tried therapy before the divorce, but this time we went conscious of our pattern, this being together, his leaving, and then my apparent inability to say no when he wanted to try again.

Our therapist was pregnant. So she kept shifting in her chair to manage the discomfort of her girth. The previous time therapy had ended with the clarity that we needed to move on. And we did. Years would pass between attempts to try again, and attempts would rarely last long enough to let others know. I spent most years as a monkish single mom, fulfilled by pour-ing out all the love that was meant for my son, whose name means "gift" in Aramaic. I did my own therapy. I even eventu-ally dated someone seriously, and felt convinced I had really moved on. But then we still found ourselves back in this same place. A different therapist, a different couch, but the same place.

She asked me, "What's the hardest part about this relation-ship?"

I took a long a time to respond. There was what I wanted to say, and there was what I hadn't said yet. What I wanted to say was what I had focused on for all these years—that his leav-ing was hardest. But now I could see what was also true, what was sitting there unsaid within me. Saying it out loud felt like lifting a heavy rock without hands for two reasons; if I said it out loud, I'd also have to own it. And it felt like the mystery that bound me to him. If I said it out loud, I would risk solving it. "What's hardest is that I keep choosing this."

She shifted again in her chair and looked over at him. I couldn't. I just stared forward like a deer caught wide-eyed in headlights, reeling with the implications of the responsibility I had just claimed. For all these years, I had focused on how to become someone he didn't want to leave—as if that would solve it. But that was never the real mystery. The real mystery meant for me was how to become someone who refuses to abandon herself.

So, at first I didn't hear anything but my own thoughts. At first I only felt the subtle vibration of our shared couch cushion start to shake slightly. Then I felt his entire body begin to tremble. And when I finally turned my head, I could see that his six-foot-six frame was curled forward over his heart, like a giant touch-me-not plant. He sobbed in that shape and told me something.

Without words, I could see radiantly clear in that moment. I saw our twinned desire, that clinging type of desire to figure out how to be together. I saw that it had him trapped in his own kind of purgatory as well.

So when I read, "Thecla did not turn back," it lit up for me like a neon sign. I knew it was time. And I also knew I couldn't do it on my own. Letting go of this love felt literally beyond me. And even though I originally wore Strong Independent Woman like a much-needed cape, over time it had morphed into armor. It clung to me like a full-body wet suit lined with duct tape.

I knew my equivalent of getting naked first meant getting sober. Which I had resisted for years because I never got drunk; I was just adept at being buzzed. So I had convinced myself that I didn't qualify. I can't claim sobriety from alcohol if I haven't felt overpowered by it. But I also knew, as a child of an alcoholic, and an avid reader of books by sober authors like Holly Whittaker's *Quit Like a Woman* and Laura McKowen's *We Are the Luckiest,* that I didn't need to be an alcoholic to have a drinking problem.

It's that when this particular form of heartbreak was loudest, the numbness some red wine at night would give me swaddled me in a layer of less feeling. It let me snuggle up again with the second power of Clinging, and just left me alone to linger there. It would let me "exist elsewhere," which is the translation of the word for death in Aramaic.

And for years, I had kept my numbing covert. I had this antique cognac snifter that I used as a wineglass. It was so small, it made my refills feel practically invisible. I kept my numbing so covert that I even kept it from myself. That is, until the night I did the splits down the hallway.

Just to give you a clearer picture. I am built as if I have two sticks of beef jerky for legs. Zero flexibility. I have two legs that were never, ever meant to assume anything even remotely close to the splits, much less for any length of time—especially not for the duration it took me to skid across the entire hallway stopped only by hitting up against the closet at the far end of it. As I was pouring my third glass of a wee bit more in the kitchen, my son meanwhile had finished his shower and scurried across the hallway floor, leaving these little grave puddles from his footsteps. So, as I made my way back to my room, my snifter full, I hit that patch of barely visible puddles and screamed a scream he still tries to imitate today as my little beef jerky legs performed the traveling splits at great speed.

I knew getting sober was the only way to get sober-sober. Meaning I couldn't heal this pattern, this compulsion, this addiction of "turning back" until I was seeing clearly, which meant being fully present within me. It meant choosing to not exist elsewhere, not even for a little bit.

The scripture reads that while Thecla is listening intently to Paul's teachings about "the divine works of Christ," her fiancé and "her own people" are searching through the streets looking for her "as one who is lost." The gatekeeper turns out to be a royal fink. He tells them that she went into the prison in order to be near Paul. And sure enough, when they go inside the prison, they find Thecla beside Paul, "bound in affection" (19:1–3).[7]

Thamyris, as we can imagine, given his temperament, was not well pleased at the sight. He went off, gathering a crowd in his rage-filled wake, and went to the governor to tell him what had happened. That Thecla, the girl he believed it was his right to marry, even though she no longer wanted to, had gone into the prison to be with Paul.

So the governor orders for both Paul and Thecla to be brought before him. The crowd calls Paul a magician again (sticks-and-stones style). The governor in seeing Thecla wants to hear from her. He wants to understand how Paul held such sway. He asks her, "Why do you not marry Thamyris according to the law of the Iconians?" (20:4). But Thecla refuses to answer, and instead, she just stands there looking intently at Paul.

Thecla is embodying something I've seen so rarely. She's saying without saying that true power means not explaining yourself. True power is trusting ourselves so completely we know no words are needed.

I've thought about this moment in the context of our modern-day lives when we make a choice that means radical change will inevitably ensue. We tend to feel the need or even the obligation to explain ourselves to those around us, especially those who don't want us to change. Often, our lives are these intricate spiderwebs. And those around us can feel this terror of a looming collapse of their own lives if we change. And what some come to understand in time, and what some never do, is that by remaining in place, each is keeping the other stuck in the invisible threads that bind them.

When we dare to be real about who we are, about what we know we're capable of doing, we trigger the egoic ties of those around us. It feels like a death for all involved. And it's only the egoic ties that break, but that's not what it feels like. It feels terrifying, and threatening. It can conjure the absolute worst version of someone we thought we knew.

When Thecla refuses to answer the governor, when she simply stands in her power for the life she has chosen by looking directly at it, the life Paul promises in Christ, her mother cries out, "Burn the lawless one! Burn the one who refuses to be a bride" (20:5).

Because of this, the governor orders for Paul to be whipped and thrown out of town, but Thecla he condemns to be burned at the stake.

When we're stripped of all these egoic identities, these titles, these names, that signify who we are, when they come crashing down in a crisis, a near-death experience, a scandal, a heartbreak, or a fire lit beneath our feet by the people we thought were our loved ones, our community, we're left exposed. We're left in a state where we no longer have a choice but to receive. Because we have nothing left outside of us. And we have nothing left covering us. There's nowhere else, and no one else to receive from now, except from within.

We've always needed for the source of love to be a presence, a witness that can never and will never leave us. A source of love that is sourced from within us. A source of love that does not and has not ever ultimately come from anyone or any single institution outside of us. A source of love that does not even recognize we are naked, that we have nothing. It's the "nothing," the lack of egoic layers, that allows the true nature of reality to arrive, to be remembered, as our own. That all we are when we have nothing left covering us is love.

We are always going to struggle with the nature of what it means to be human if we refuse to walk through the terror of this scene, of Thecla's naked vulnerability at the loss of all the names and titles that had before given her life meaning. We can't allow ourselves to change without first having the humility to see it, the need for change. For growth.

The power in being naked, of being stripped of all the identities we wear, is that we are then in a state of vulnerability. And vulnerability has been so feared and misunderstood as a weakness, as something to avoid at all costs. But there's a power in that level of authenticity.

When we are vulnerable, we are only relying on what's left, and what's left is the truth, and what's true comes from within. There's nothing covering us; not someone else's belief or thought or theory about us.

Nakedness is a rite of passage. It's compulsory for birth. And it's the only way we can begin again, as someone new, or as more of the truth of who we are, more authentic, more real. We have to get naked willingly or by waiting for the whispers of the need to change to morph into a roar. Whether the nakedness feels forced by external circumstances or initiated by conscious intention, the nakedness means we're ready to begin again. But first comes death.

THE FIFTH STAGE

So we're often asked at some point to die. To go through a death that will mean a return is no longer possible, or at least that we can never return to what used to be, to who we used to be. We become someone new, which is terrifying. And if we can survive the death, if we can survive the terror of becoming someone unalterably new, we inherit power. Deep, true power. Power that only comes from within. This is the fifth stage. It's when all the perceived losses, and all the suffering, begin to transform into what the alchemists toiled away toward: gold.

17.

Death

And the young men and young women brought firewood and straw so that Thecla might be burned. And as she came naked, the governor wept and marveled at the power in her. And the executioners laid out the firewood and ordered her to climb upon the pyre. And when she made the sign of the cross, she climbed upon the firewood. They lit it and a great fire blazed, but the fire did not touch her.

—*The Acts of Paul and Thecla* 22:1–4

Scripture is revealed. Meaning scripture must be interpreted. It must be filtered through the lens of lived experience. It can be as easily used to justify hate as it is to glorify liberation.

If you give me Leviticus 18 written centuries before the first century C.E., "You shall not lie with a man as a woman," to justify homophobia or transphobia in the twenty-first century, I'll give you John 13 with the commandment that we are to love one another as Christ loved—meaning radically, unconditionally. If you give me 1 Timothy 2, "I do not consent to them becoming teachers, or exercising authority over men;

they ought not speak," to embolden sexism, to sanctify violence against women and girls—silencing us, keeping us from
education, from positions of political and spiritual authority—
I'll give you Galatians 3:28, where there is neither male nor
female, Jew nor Greek, slave nor free, "For you are all one in
Christ."[1] And if you give me Ephesians 6, "Slaves obey your
earthly masters," to deify racism, oppression, and subjugation,
I'll give you Galatians 5:13, where we're reminded that we've
all been called here to be free, and that the "whole Law" is
summed up in this one precept: "You must love your neighbor
as you love yourself."[2]

What's the missing element in an exegete who reads hate
where I read liberation? The heart—the "greatest of these"
from 1 Corinthians 13:13.[3] Not faith. Not hope. Love. Love is
the greatest of these three enduring aspects of humanity, because it is the lens; it is the hermeneutic through which I believe scripture is meant to be read and interpreted. Because
only love undresses the ego.

What can't be underestimated is the death that's required
in order to pass through the threshold, so that an actual new
life for us can begin. A new life that means we can never return
to our previous way of being in the world.

Let's try to imagine together what this moment was like for
Thecla. She has been sentenced by the governor to burn at the
stake, a suggestion made by her own mother. Her community,
even the young people her own age within it, have gathered
to either participate in her execution or to stand as spectators
on the sidelines and say nothing as she burns. Thecla has been
stripped. And as an act of public shaming, she has to walk
through the crowd toward the executioner completely naked.
As feminist theorist bell hooks explains, "Shaming is one of
the deepest tools of the imperialist, white supremist, capitalist

patriarchy because shame produces trauma and trauma often produces paralysis."[4]

Thecla scours the crowd like "a lamb in the wilderness" (21:3),[5] trying to find Paul's face as she walks toward the pyre. Paul has already been beaten and banished. But Thecla still finds him among the passive, complicit mass of people, because as the scripture explains, Christ appears to her in Paul's form. Thecla says to herself, "As if I were not able to endure, Paul has come to see me" (21:4).[6] Once Thecla's eyes land on Christ appearing as Paul, she stares at him intently. And that look of love, that presence of love when love is most needed; this is the light that we can meet with once we've stripped off everything we used to be. Because now we are no longer wearing any expectations others might have of us or any conditions in order to be loved.

This look of love is the confirmation of love's unconditional design. And when it meets us there, in that state of vulnerability, there's a power we inherit, or that we remember that no one and nothing outside of us can ever take from us. We are indelibly changed from that look of love when everyone else has left us. When all the reasons we thought we were loved, or deserved to be loved, have been stripped from us. When we are being brutally misunderstood, when we are being crucified by those even that we once called family. When we are at our most bleak, at the utter depths of what it means to be human, and that look of love still meets us there, we merge with a truth that has walked with us. When love witnesses us there, we can finally see what love sees in us—that we are just this solitary soul behind these very human eyes.

And that look of love is reciprocated. Or this is how I see it. Thecla sees Paul seeing her. She sees that she is beloved to that one pair of eyes she cares about most. She sees that here in this moment when everyone else has abandoned her, love is her witness. That even when everyone has betrayed her, from the systems of power within her home and family to the systems of power in the government, when everyone has failed to see the light that's right there behind her eyes, behind her gender, behind her body; even when all those systems of power have failed to protect her, or worse, have sacrificed her for the sake of maintaining a status quo, love doesn't leave her.

Mary Magdalene never left Christ's side all during the crucifixion and the three days and three nights before the resurrection. We know this from the texts that were included in the traditional Christian canon; Mary Magdalene was there at the empty tomb to tend to his body, and to find out where his body had been taken.

I've wondered if Mary was also with him from within her, as if they were tethered together with an unseen thread that their human love, whatever its nature, created. Like Ariadne's red thread leading Theseus through the unlit labyrinth, maybe Mary's love for Christ gave him a ballast, a trail of breadcrumbs, to find his way consciously through death back to this realm where her love for him remained. Their love was maybe an anchor, an echo he could follow through the redemption of death back to the world where she existed. I've never believed, not for a moment, even as a little girl, that Mary Magdalene just happened to be there at the empty tomb. That it was a "right time, right place" situation. Mary was there because she was Christ's witness. Just as Paul is Thecla's in her moment of death. Because love is a witness.

I've often imagined the power of this moment when Mary witnessed Christ's resurrection and when Christ witnessed Mary's embodiment of his teachings by the fact that she could see him.

Thecla is being fully seen and fully known in this moment of her death. She's being met "face-to-face" with love. And this is what I think Exodus 33:20 means: "You cannot see my face, for no one may see my face and live." We don't survive being fully seen by love. We die because of it. We can no longer return to the life we had before it. Because the life we knew before this look of love, this seeing and being seen by god, is no longer viable. This is why I think, when Thecla walked naked through the crowd, "the governor wept and marveled at the power in her" (22:2).[7] It's a power he has never seen embodied before. And it's a power more tremendous than his own. Because it's a power that resides within her; it's not bestowed on her by external forces, but sourced from within her own heart.

Thecla had nothing left to hide. And she had no one there for her, no friend or ally willing to help her. She had no value to the world around her except as an example of what not to do, except to be used as a pawn of terror for those girls around her who might decide to free themselves as she had of the expectation to be owned by a man.

The scripture says that after Thecla looks intently at Christ in Paul's form, "he departed into heaven" (21:4).[8] For me, this passage suggests that when it seems others are determined to misunderstand you, when you've been humbled, exposed, and when you're convinced that you're alone, heaven threads itself into that moment to witness you, to be with you, to remind you that there is no place you can ever go or be taken where love cannot reach you.

Then the executioners order Thecla to climb onto the pyre. And as she climbs up on the firewood, she makes the sign of the cross. A gesture of her resolve. Fear has not won today. I die with my faith still with me, sheltering me, Thecla says wordlessly.

And just as the flames begin to build, the scripture reads, "God, having compassion, caused a sound under the earth, and a cloud, filled with rain and hail, darkened the sky from above, and the vessel poured forth all that was in it" (22:4).[9] Some sort of earthquake and a sudden torrential downpour converge so that the fire meant to kill Thecla is extinguished, and Thecla is saved.

Thecla climbs down from the pyre and leaves what had been her home. Thecla leaves the self her community had sacrificed on that pyre, and climbs down from it as only the true self that survived it.

When I think of the death that Christ went through, that Mary witnessed, it seems to address this question: Where has our love not yet reached? Christ had experienced directly all that needed to be touched, redeemed in life by love. And if Christ came to redeem humanity, or if Christ came to let love reach where it has never been before, then of course he would have to bring love even to death, all the way through it, and back again.

The first name Christ said when he resurrected was "Mary." He said her name and only then, once she heard her name in his voice, did she recognize that it was Christ, and not the gardener. He made it out through the labyrinth and back again. He brought love to where it had never been before, and he rose again in order to meet it, face-to-face. So that the power of human love could be witnessed.

If we take the resurrection narrative metaphorically, and if we see Thecla's moment of emerging through the flames un-scathed as symbolic, then the spiritual practice of *kenosis* comes into view. The practice of emptying the false ideas we hold about ourselves, or the ones others have projected onto us, the practice of dying to who we used to be, or even who we used to tolerate being sometimes for the sake of others, in order to emerge as a truer version of ourselves. And by "truer," I just mean a more transparent human being. Where what's within us is who we share.

The church, I think, was always meant to die metaphorically. To keep releasing old ideas of itself again and again, making itself new. Rising to meet a bolder, more embodied love each time. Rising to meet each next awareness of where love has not yet reached. As a theologian and a seminarian, I was led course after course through the ways the church formed from the fourth century onward. And how it fractured and splintered and transplanted cuttings, like pruning from the roots, and grew new species of churches in separate pots. How do we build a church with roots that extend down, or back and through, to the Christ Movement that existed before it?

The pandemic was a global death, a collective death. It was a literal and a metaphoric death for the majority of us. It was a time when so much of what we thought mattered, so much of who we thought we were or had to be, died.

The most effectual therapy for me includes the body. Healing modalities that can reach where trauma is stored in the body, like EMDR (eye movement desensitization and reprocessing), have transformed my PTSD from sexual assault and the subsequent anxiety disorder I have managed most of my life. So, in order to get sober-sober, to no longer "turn back," a close friend suggested a somatic coach who specializes in trauma resolution. Somatic therapy is a body-centric approach to healing mental health issues. I felt a resounding *yes* even before I knew her name, which means in Greek "reaching out over a great distance."

The night after our first session, I felt like a mollusk who had been deshelled. And without my wee bit more in my little snifter, there was no buffer.

I texted my friend, author and spiritual teacher Gabby Bernstein, only wanting to tiptoe into asking for help, but she immediately FaceTimed me. Which felt like the equivalent of all the alarms in a fire station going off at once inside my body. I froze. Hands shaking. Then I answered, and Strong Independent Woman was yanked off me—with a layer of skin—in that one excruciating second.

I will always remember what that conversation felt like. Because, when I answered, I felt like a Sith Lord from *Star Wars* in my hooded sweatshirt. But what I met with when that FaceTime screen opened to her expression was not one of horror looking at the absolute least lovable version of me; instead, she was aggressively radiating compassion at me, with a love that loved me, even that form of me that was writhing in pain.

And this is what marked the end of my turning back. This exact exchange. Of feeling worthy enough to no longer want to suffer, and being vulnerable enough to ask for help. Because this is the moment we give others the chance to be there for us, to be a love that can meet us where our own love for ourselves hasn't reached yet.

I restarted the show I had been watching before texting her, which I wasn't paying much attention to until, yep, that phrase found me. "The definition of insanity is doing the same thing over and over and expecting different results."

And again, like every other time I had encountered it, I just knew. *I knew.* It was like Vanna White walking very elegantly across my field of vision and turning over the truth. There was no judgment. There was only this searing clarity that this pattern is about the power to choose. It's about finding and then

flexing a discrete muscle I didn't yet feel consciously connected to.

There's this moment I love in *The Gospel of Mary* when the
seven powers of the ego interrogate the soul by asking, "Where
are you coming from, human-killer, and where are you going,
space-conqueror?" (9:26).[10] The powers of the ego are so
threatened by the love the soul contains that they resort to
name-calling. It's a love that can "kill" the ego, and it's a love
that "conquers" or transcends space and time, because it's infinite, eternal. It's a love that can reach back from the present
moment and heal what we could never figure out how to heal
in the past.

I recently had a conversation about neuroplasticity with
wellness expert Ruby Jusas, and she summarized it all so suc-
cinctly: "Anything that is familiar to the brain is seen as safe,
even if it is harmful or not what we want. Our brain is capable
of learning the habit of pain."

Several sessions later, somatic therapy with "reaching out
over a great distance" kept bringing me back to a vivid memory of a time when my dad drove me to his house after my
parents' divorce, a memory that I had never forgotten or re-
pressed. I just couldn't connect to it, or feel anything about it,
even though it seemed to live within me as if in present tense.

I watch my little seven-year-old hand grab the interior door
handle in the passenger seat of his car as he races up a steep
hill. I know he's drunk from the amount of cologne he's wearing. Then he suddenly swerves out across the double yellow
line to overtake a truck that's moving too slowly. We stay on
the wrong side of the road as he makes the sharp right turn
blindly and speeds past the truck at the top of the hill. Terror
hits me so completely there's a high-pitched ringing noise in
my body. I keep staring at my hand as if from a great distance

even though it's right here in front of me. I witness it, as if it isn't mine anymore. And I can't move, for a long time, even once the car stops. I remain at a great distance from everything.

And from this distance, I can feel a giant vat of love for me within him, an unconditional love he would give unfalteringly once sober. So despite his actions, I remain devoted to him. And this pain of abandonment, of my dad choosing alcohol before my safety, this is "home" to me. And the cost of staying home means abandoning my own body. This is what I was replicating in my never-ending marriage.

This was the thing itself. And this is what this love for my son's dad was always meant to do. It wasn't the love story I had wanted. But it was the singular love that could break my heart so exquisitely, and with such precision, that it led me back to this scene. To this first moment when I left myself. And this was the moment that held the key. Here in my body, tucked away for all these years, until I had become the love that could witness it.

For all these years, I had wanted him to become what I needed to be for myself: a love that doesn't leave.

This was the thing itself. And once I went through that same memory, now embodied with the look of love only I could bring it, the weight of mercy pulled me under. Mercy met with this first moment I "existed elsewhere," and then swept through every inch of me, every story. Mercy crowded out all the anguish, the years of trying so hard to hear and be heard, years of wishing our lives could be different. Mercy pitched a tent for me inside my heart, handed me a stethoscope to press to the walls of it, and sat with me as I listened for longer than it felt good to, until I heard all that this heart of mine had clung to.

And the exchange felt something like this: I gave up everything I had been holding on to, everything I thought I needed, all that I had suffered and lost, every word of it, and what came back poured out from within me. A love that extended out to the family I was born into and to the family I had made, and tried to remake. A love that freed me by giving it. A love that released mercy like oxygen into my bloodstream. For everything I felt I should have done better, and for all the shame I felt for not healing sooner. So much mercy poured through me for being Herman for so long, it's still spilling out through my eyes as I write this.

Maybe all the cages, the confining attic spaces, the redbrick houses the ego creates for us have always in the end been unlocked from the inside. Mercy is the word that freed me from mine.

This spiritual practice of the kenotic path, of releasing the egoic powers, relies on our capacity to recognize them. I had heard repeatedly from readers over the years wanting to know more about the seven powers after encountering *The Gospel of Mary*. Because they are translated from the Greek and Coptic in her gospel in ways that are hard to grasp. Also, it has been a millennia and a half since Pope Gregory, Cassian, and Evagrius took a turn at interpreting the list; I figured it was time to offer a feminist one.

I focused on refining and reframing the powers so they make sense to us in the modern world. This also gave me a chance to continue to work on them personally. For the next several years, I worked on an oracle deck that included them so that I could offer this same spiritual practice to anyone who wants to do the sober-sobering work of getting spiritually naked.[11]

The first power in *The Gospel of Mary* is "darkness," which is straightforward, so it remained Darkness. Darkness is ultimately when we believe so fully in the illusion that we're separate—we feel it so entirely that we think we're alone. We feel not just bereft of others, not just lonely, but also without hope of feeling connected to someone again. And that's the hardest part of sitting in the dark, not realizing how many others are sitting right there in the darkness with us. An inch away even. So what we can work on in this power is the inner vision that Darkness makes possible.

The second power is described as "desire." But desire can be salvific, revolutionary even. There's a fierce radiant ember that lives inside us, like a true north. And this core of who we really are is meant to be nurtured into its fullest expression. Maybe it's just significant here to distinguish between an egoic desire versus what the soul desires. Or maybe it's because being in my body enough to know what I actually desire feels like a triumph, a perseverance of spirit, not a power of the ego.

For all these reasons, I renamed desire "Clinging." Because this is the challenge this power provides us as human beings; it's the kind of desire that comes from the ego clinging to what we think we need, and when we think we're supposed to get it. It's wishing other people could be someone else. It's wishing we were someone else. It's clinging to outcomes and timelines. It's clinging to who we think we should be rather than accepting and seeing the truth of who we are now in this moment.

The third power is listed as "ignorance." Ignorance is clear like Darkness, so I also kept it the same. We all experience it in ourselves and others so frequently. It's the classic inability to see ourselves fully, to only focus on what's wrong with others and not what might need to be healed in or changed about ourselves. It's the obliviousness in Luke 6 about wanting to remove a splinter from someone else's eye without noticing the wooden beam sticking out of our own. Ignorance is marked by a profound lack of vision. Ignorance is the lack of self-awareness to see the impact of our actions. And it's the inability to see the actual interconnectedness of all that exists. So the medicine in this power is in acquiring right relation to all things; it's the humility in knowing no one, human or angel, is greater or less than another.

Powers four through six are all about our relationship to the body. They highlight the importance of embodiment. Yet they are worded in confusing ways in the original translation from the Greek, so I spent the most time on them. So first there's Darkness, then Clinging, and next Ignorance. The fourth power is described in *The Gospel of Mary* as the "eagerness for death." This is the power that is centuries later named within the church's delineation of the seven deadly sins as "gluttony."

For me, it's a power of the ego, not a sin, when we are compelled to consume excessive amounts of anything. It's consuming a harmful and dangerous amount of any kind of substance, or going to such an extreme that we actually threaten our health and longevity. We sacrifice the health of our body when this power holds us captive. So I renamed the fourth power "Excess." Excess allows us to learn to use the word "beloved" as a ballast within us when we start to tilt toward an extreme. That we are beloved, without condition, is our anchor; it can slow the gravitational pull toward an extreme or drag us back from it. Because it is the truest truth.

The fifth power is "the realm of the flesh." This later is renamed as the sin of "lust" within the Church's concept of the seven deadly sins. As someone who has spent decades learning to heal the need to disassociate, finding a hard-won embodiment and remaining even during an argument, even during a panic attack, even during sex, "the realm of the flesh" sounds like a New Year's resolution. Sounds like the name of a true guru. Sounds like the entire point.

The challenge that the fifth power is communicating in *The Gospel of Mary* is that we can forget that we are also a soul. We are a body and a soul both, simultaneously. When we mistake the body as our true self, and all that we can cleave to and crave, and need and want, then we are trapped in the fifth power. And when we approach someone or see and treat them as if they are just a body, we harm not only their body but also their relationship to it, and their capacity to exist within it. So I renamed the fifth power "Forgetting." We get the opportunity with this power, each time we forget, to remember that the body is the soul's chance to be here.

The sixth power according to *The Gospel of Mary* is "the foolish wisdom of the flesh." As a scholar of the history of women in religion, my hackles go up immediately with this description. To call the flesh foolish is to suggest that the flesh matters less than the soul. In my direct experience, the body has wisdom no scripture can teach. No matter how holy the book, how sacred the scripture, nothing can compete with the revelation of just being fully present in the body. The body is a barometer of truth. And women throughout the history of world religions have been scapegoated disproportionately for this glaringly unresolved issue religion has with sex and sexuality.

The body doesn't lie.

This is what I've learned—listening to the way the body

speaks to me is a form of devotion. Listening inwardly to how the body informs me from the moment I first meet someone, or first walk into a room or start a conversation, my body is speaking volumes of silent, unfiltered truth. So I named the sixth power "The Body."

The seventh power is "wrathful wisdom," which sounds sardonic. So I named the seventh power simply "Rage." Similar to Clinging versus desire, there's a need to clarify that there's a rage that love inspires that serves as information, and there's a rage that seeks to destroy. And understanding the distinction between the two is the difference between healing and remaining in the grip of suffering.

There's a rage that gives us clarity about when our boundaries are being crossed, a rage that gives us critical information that we're in danger, that someone is harming us or someone we love. There's a rage that demonstrates to us how interconnected we are, for example when we feel rage while witnessing an injustice. Rage makes palpable for us that, as author Glennon Doyle frequently puts it, "There's no such thing as other people's children."

Seeing George Floyd murdered was something we all witnessed collectively because seventeen-year-old Darnella Frazier refused to leave his side, refused to listen to the police officers who told her to move on, and instead remained, and filmed on her iPhone the murder that would reignite social justice movements all over the globe. This form of rage is sacred. It's a rage that clarifies what we care most about in this world, about what we will put our bodies on the line to stand up for.

The distinction is that we let this sacred rage motivate us into action, but when we act we move from love. The rage that *The Gospel of Mary* lists as the seventh power is the rage that seeks to destroy ourselves and others. It's the rage of revenge.

The rage of trying to get even. It's the rage of an endless cycle of retaliation. It's the rage that can compel us to act in ways we will regret for the rest of our lives, or that will cost us our lives or someone else's. It's the rage that refuses mercy. It's the rage that keeps us up at night locked in a horrific egoic struggle going over again and again a betrayal, a terrible wrong someone has caused us.

And it's a rage that thinks it's right, which I suppose is "wrathful wisdom." The rage comes from this place of feeling justified. That we have every right to cause harm to someone who has harmed us. That we have every right to get all caught up in the ego, in our own tiny window of perception about some person, that we get to take our rage out on them.

These powers are listed in *The Gospel of Mary* so that they are discernible to us. They are powers or "climates," as author Cynthia Bourgeault refers to them, that we are meant to encounter. They are not listed here to shame us, to make us feel unworthy, or guilty for experiencing them. The whole point is to become more and more aware of the way these powers surface in our lives every day, and then do the work that lets us die to them. So we can meet face-to-face with love again. This is the practice—die to the egoic self, and let the soul supersede it. Not at the end of this life, when we no longer have this chance at embodiment, but now, while we still can.

I think every person, every institution, every church is meant to undergo some version of this ancient kenotic path, this path of love. So we don't mistake the ego for god.

In their original form in *The Gospel of Mary,* the seven powers are not a critique of humanity; they're simply information, listed in a non-judgy form of what we'll encounter while in the human body. They're critical information about our relationship to being human. They're meant to help us become increasingly aware of when one of these powers of the ego has us enthralled. So that we can practice bringing love within us to where it has never reached before.

If these seven powers exist within us, within every human being, then they also exist within everything we create. No matter how sacred and exceptional. No matter how powerful and successful, and maybe especially then. The seven powers are there. And the whole point is to have the humility and the mercy to be able to see the power of the ego that might be guiding our choices. The whole point is to not cover it up with hubris, or a black leather jacket. The point is to bring it out into the light.

Here's what happens when we die to a power of the ego— we suffer the loss of an illusion about ourselves, an illusion that we believed made us worthy of love. We suffer the loss of an identity that was actually never large enough to contain us. Here's what happens when we die to the ego—we believe we have lost what was most valuable only to finally see that the real gold, the immovable love we sought outside us, was sitting unrealized underneath it all, right here within.

The systemic abuses of power within the church are rooted into the foundation of the church. Not with Christ but with Constantine. And this original collusion of Christ with empire, with a name that should signify love and instead often wields a misuse of power, has remained ever since. The hierarchy established within the church under Constantine meant that a priest, and later a pastor, an elder, a minister, an authority of any kind within the church, had power *over* the congregation. Just as the emperor had power *over* his subjects. We are to be submissive to them as we are to be submissive to a ruler, and to god.

Throughout the history of Christianity, hundreds of thousands of lives have been forever changed because church leaders and congregants chose to be spectators, chose to remain silent rather than become witnesses, rather than do the hard work of letting love finally reach to the most wounded and most wounding places of the church.

From the atrocities coming to light about the global scale of child sexual assault throughout the Catholic Church, to the scandals shuttering the Pentecostal church Hillsong, to the horrific abuse of an entire generation of Native American children in Christian boarding schools, we have to witness the egoic tendency for the church to protect the perpetrator, to mitigate the financial impact on the community, to care more about the scandal the truth will bring rather than the current and future harm being caused to those abused.

How do we dismantle the systematic abuse of power that is embedded into the codification of the New Testament itself? Revealed by the fact that the very systems that may have held that power in check, the positions of authority held by women in the Christ Movement, and the scriptures that pointed us to a "royal power" within us, were excluded from it, ordered to be destroyed, and buried in the Egyptian desert. How do we remind ourselves and our children that no one, ever, has the right to wield power over us? Not even, or especially, those wearing the clothes of "god"?

We are evolving. Or so this is the faith, the hope I have in humanity. That we are dying to intolerance, hate, racism, sexism, homophobia, bigotry in all its forms. That we are in each next version of ourselves, and in each next generation taking on the unbearable weight of seeing how much as humans we're responsible for, and of just how much we need to listen. Not just to the ego but also to the heart. Not just to the true self but also to the collective. Not only to fear but especially to love.

Love does not ever seek to dominate or control but to be with all that is. And it's the being *with* us that changes us. It's the witnessing that transforms everything. It's the presence of love that turns a death, an "existing elsewhere," into a resurrection, and transforms a murderous pyre into the bonfire of our next incarnation.

18.

Prayer

And Thecla said to Paul, "I will cut my hair short and follow you wherever you go." But he said, "It is a shameful time and you are fair. May no other trial come upon you worse than the first, and this time you are not able to stand firm but are cowardly." And Thecla said, "Only give me the seal of Christ and no trial will touch me."

—*The Acts of Paul and Thecla* 25:3–5

Written evidence of Hesychasm, an ancient contemplative tradition within Christianity, dates back to as early as the fourth century based on spiritual manuscripts from Egypt, among them John Cassian's *Institutes.* He's attributed with transmitting these teachings to the West, when he traveled from Egypt and settled in France. The spiritual practice of the Hesychasts is a form of inner prayer that clarifies the heart in the *Purgatio* stage, or in Greek *Catharsis.* The word "Hesychasm" comes from the Greek *hesychia,* which means "stillness, silence, or rest," and translates directly as "to keep stillness."

I focused my research in seminary on this mystical tradition, both as a scholar and a practitioner, because the Hesychasts wrote from direct experience of the *nous*—which we know is what Christ refers to in *The Gospel of Mary* as "the treasure" (7:4).[1] The Greek word *nous,* or eye of the heart, is the treasure because this is the aperture that allows for direct knowing—so we can discern between what's ego and what's the calm, still voice of love within us.

It's the form of spiritual vision we can acquire, once we clarify the heart through meditation. In a compilation of writings by Hesychasts, Saint Isaac of Syria advises, "Try to enter your inner treasure-house and you will see the treasure-house of heaven."[2] The Trappist monk Thomas Merton describes the *nous* as "a pure diamond, blazing with the invisible light of heaven."[3]

The essence of the *nous* is ultimately to serve as a meeting ground within us where the finite and the infinite meet. It's an aspect of the soul that we can learn to perceive by focusing all of our consciousness into the heart during meditation. It is not the soul; it's like a window into it. It's like a Magic 8 Ball hidden deep in the body. Remember Christ's response to Mary's question about how she was able to perceive a vision: "One does not see with the soul or with the spirit, but the mind which is between the two sees the vision" (7:6–7).[4] The mind, or the *nous* here, then, is uniquely human. It's how we can recognize the egoic layers we need to release, strip off. The *nous* is what makes kenosis possible. It's not the soul or the spirit but what exists between them. And this is what I found so fascinating—this mystical union with *nous,* with this window to what's true and real and lasting for us, takes place not by leaving, transcending, or ignoring the body, but by learning to become fully present within it.

In the thirteenth century, Saint Nicephorus the Hesychast

added a psychosomatic technique to the inner prayer through the use of a yogic posture of curling forward over the heart.

So when I trained in seminary as a modern-day Hesychast, I was instructed to curve the top half of my body into an inglorious C, and to physically direct all of my mental focus into the center of my chest, while repeating inwardly *Kyrie eleison,* which is Greek for "Lord, have mercy." My body began to protest, though, very eloquently when I curled forward for hours on end. So I opted instead to pray as the earlier Hesychasts had. Especially since the transformation the inner prayer was creating for me came from the word "mercy." Mercy feels imbued with a power that extends back to antiquity, as if an all-consuming fire, that accepts and transforms everything, is handed to me in that single word, that generations of mystics have kept lit from the countless times it was repeated within them.

Over time, I continued to make the practice my own, referring to it as the soul-voice meditation. Sometimes it's as quick and simple as taking three intentional breaths: one to return to the heart, one to merge with the love that waits there, and one to return, hopefully seeing more with the vision that's possible then, once consciousness is anchored back into the heart. Sometimes it's a much longer meditation, because with that second breath, I stay still in the heart and pray from there, which is often about asking questions and listening in the silence for what might surface.

A professor of mine from Harvard, Dr. Jeffrey Kripal, practiced and taught a form of mystical hermeneutics, illuminating the ways in which reading a sacred text can elicit mystical experiences in order for the spiritual teachings in the text to be acquired not through the intellect, but rather through direct experience. He suggests, "I think there is something cosmic or superhuman smoldering in the human, something that seems ready to burst into flames, and sometimes does."[5] He created the Archives of the Impossible at Rice University to keep a record of just how often the "impossible" is a part of what it means to be human; with near-death experiences, encounters with loved ones who have passed, people who appear as if "angels" and then disappear, and seemingly superhuman capacities like levitation, telepathy, and precognition.

This is all a prelude to tell you about the other form of prayer that has constellated my life. The form of prayer that's more like being prayed through. My knees sort of cease to function, and I drop down to the ground. Or if I'm near a bed, I spread out over it. And it's not pretty. This is not that classic image of the small figurine with her hands pressed together under her chin in prayer and a serene smile on her face. This is more reminiscent of post-wrestling match, with my whole midsection sprawled out over the top of my comforter and my arms stretched out to either side as if I'd just fallen from the ceiling.

And then from this unknowable core of my frame, I pray. And the words rush through me in this "thy will be done" tone. It's a tone I don't use outside of prayer. It's in the imperative mood. It's very lady boss. Which struck me as odd the first time it happened. I was a neophyte pilgrim traveling alone to various Black Madonnas in the South of France after graduating from divinity school. I found myself in the small side chapel at the cathedral in Le Puy, France. From researching the mystic Simone Weil, I knew that she had visited that chapel, and had prayed to that same Black Madonna. I thought about the outsiders we are to the church, and yet the twin pull we've had toward a Christ that loves even what we cannot love.

As I was meditating, a weight came over me. I felt as heavy as lead. I went down like a flour sack onto the carpeted aisle of the chapel. And the voice that came through me had a confidence I had never heard in myself. It was this voice that was filled with both love and knowing. Both ease and certainty. It was a voice that knew the worth of what it means to be human. So when the voice within me said, "Show me the way," it wasn't with the tone I use when I'm asking. It wasn't an ask. It was a directive. A demand. An essential requirement. As if I were a scuba diver, and I had just "asked" for the equipment needed to breathe underwater.

Years later, when I was studying the New Testament in depth at seminary, I was relieved to find that this lady boss tone is common when it comes to prayer. For example, Christ in the Gospel of John appeals to god on behalf of the disciples: "Make them holy in truth."[6] The imperative tense is used in his prayer. Infused within the ask is this trust that what is being asked for is already answered. There isn't a "will you, please, pretty please" energy to the ask. It's more an ask that is a description of what's going to happen. There's no room for negotiation. It's this gorgeous command laced with gratitude and awareness that the purpose in being human is to practice being this bridge, as a voice between the seen and the unseen, between the manifested world and the world that might yet still manifest. Paul uses this same imperative mood in *The Acts of Paul and Thecla*.

Mary Magdalene's encounter with the risen Christ comes at the *empty* tomb. For Thecla, after she sees Christ in Paul's form before climbing onto the pyre, she arrives at the *open* tomb—where Paul has been praying, along with Onesie's whole family, including Lectra and the kids. One of their children went to the market to get bread and ran into Thecla. He recognized her as his neighbor from home. Thecla tells him that she has been searching for Paul since she survived the fire. And then he says, "I will lead you to him for he is mourning for you and has been praying and fasting for six days already" (23:7).[7]

When Thecla arrives at the open tomb, Paul is kneeling and praying, in that lady boss tone, "Do not let the fire touch Thecla, but stand by her because she is yours" (24:1).[8] Thecla realizes in this moment that Paul's prayer was answered, that all along through that entire "death" she endured, she had been connected to him in prayer. Paul's human love for Thecla, his prayer from the heart for her, rips open the fabric of reality, or the reality of what we expect normalcy to hold each day. Paul had prayed himself beside her.

After Thecla locks eyes with Christ in Paul's form, and after they exchange that look of love as she's forced to walk naked toward the pyre, the scripture reads, "And she looked intently at him; but he departed into heaven" (21:4).[9] So human love can bring the things of heaven here to be with us, to assist us with the impossible, to help us exist for others in places we couldn't possibly be.

Paul's tone is that same imperative mood that comes through me when I am prayed. A sharing of what will happen, in love's name—"Do not let the fire touch Thecla," Paul prays.

Let's magnify the beauty that Paul prayed himself beside Thecla—that Christ appeared in Paul's form so that Thecla knew in that moment when she was most alone, abandoned by everyone who had ever said they loved her, that true love remained. Christ didn't appear as himself, toting a shepherd's staff or bursting with rays. Christ took the form that would comfort Thecla the most, that would signify love the most for her, and that would allow her to embody it. Christ took the human form of the one praying his little angelic face off for her several towns over in an open tomb.

So when I prayed during the pandemic, it wasn't pretty. It was sprawled out, it was wet-faced, it was lady boss gone feral. I kept stillness, like the Hesychasts, and put mercy on repeat within me. I knew my prayers would be answered just as I knew those answered prayers wouldn't appear in the way my ego might imagine. We can ask with the saltiest imperative mood we can conjure, and we will receive what we pray for. Answered prayers just rarely arrive in the way the ego desires or pictures. And sometimes what we pray for is replaced by a prayer we could never have conjured on our own. Sometimes we don't even know the kind of death we just walked through until someone loves us back to life.

With all the events canceled for my book about *The Gospel of Mary*, I had this unprecedented time to respond to readers. There was a common thread that ran through so many, which went something like—"finding Mary's gospel reminded me of the Christ I knew before I went to church."

There was one from a priest in a monastery who always believed there was more to Mary's story. There was one from a survivor of conversion therapy who said finding *The Gospel of Mary* was critical to healing. And there were countless messages relating that I had put into words what so many had intuitively known, that Mary was something so much more provocative than a prostitute.

And then, there was a message from a man who introduced himself as a songwriter and queer storyteller. His words about my book on Mary hit me different. It was like searching for a radio station—I could hear his words suddenly as I read them like that split second when the static morphs into the frequency of music: "The moment it was in my hands it was like holding an uncovered power, like breathing in the air of a basilica." With this one sentence, with the love he tucked inside it, I got the "why" that's at the root of all I do—for this precise transference of power—this memory that the most sacred form of it is already ours. He attached a song he had written, titled "Mother, Mary, and Me." A song about letting go of everything we think we need. And when I listened to it, I felt this uncanny sense that we already knew each other. Let's call him Jacob from the bible.

Political analyst and civil rights activist Van Jones sent encouraging words about my work of unearthing women's spiritual voices. He connected me to Rahiel Tesfamariam, a public minister and liberation theologian who had been arrested alongside Dr. Cornel West in Ferguson. And the three of us began to imagine together a virtual space where anyone could go to be spiritually fed. We named it MANNA. Then artist and activist Lilakoi Moon joined us, and as a quaternity, we wove together our concern for the earth, for prison reform, for the voices of women, and especially women of color in positions of spiritual authority. We prayed for and with each other. And this is when I finally began to understand Lazarus, what it means to be loved back to life.

A miracle is defined as an inexplicable surprise, a welcome and yet improbable event. According to *A Course in Miracles,* a miracle is a shift in our perception. A miracle comes as a sign that we're seeing or perceiving the presence of love more clearly. The miracles begin in Thecla's story as soon as she walks through the metaphorical death, as soon as she dies to all the egoic ties that had bound her to the life she was born into, the life that was expected of her. The first miracle: An extraordinarily well-timed storm puts out the flames lit beneath her feet. And as we soon discover, the miraculous is inextricably linked to the human endeavor of ardent prayer.

The first miracle I experienced didn't appear to be a miracle at all. I only recognized it in retrospect. It was an inexplicable surprise, though, and a highly improbable event. It was markedly different from the storm that arrives to save Thecla's life, but it was a flood of sorts. And it was such an outrageous sign, it set my life on course correct. There was a place in the South my family had visited for decades, where my body just exhaled, and claimed as home. In the wake of "the miracle," my son and his dad, whose name means "god will increase," suggested we take this as our cue to finally move there. An act of love that shocked me in the moment and still feeds me in this one.

The first miracle: In the middle of the night, out of nowhere, a horrific gurgling sound came from the pipes. All the pipes. From the toilets, the sinks, and the shower drains. An epic force was brewing, so I darted frantically between my bathroom and my son's bathroom trying not to know what I knew was about to happen. It was just too unthinkable. And when the flood came, when the shower, bathtub, and toilets were all overflowing my apartment with sewage, from a clogged pipe that had burst in the unit above me, all I could do was keep repeating the title of my friend Robert Holden's book, a sort of greatest hits from *A Course in Miracles,* titled *Holy Shift.*

When Paul sees that Thecla survived the fire, that what he had been praying and fasting six days for was answered on the seventh day, Thecla is there standing before him. The scripture reads, "And there was much love in the tomb" (25:1).[10] Paul breaks his fast with the loaves of bread that the young boy bought at the market. They break bread together, and they swap stories about "the divine works of Christ" (25:2).[11]

Now that Thecla has died and become someone new, now that her heart is clear, she knows she is as worthy as Paul to teach about Christ. So, she suggests to him, "I will cut my hair short and follow you wherever you go" (25:3).[12] This is significant first because she is the one to initiate what her life will look like now. She is unafraid to tell Paul what she wants. It's also significant because hair length held meaning in the first century—short hair was worn solely by men and signified intelligence, whereas women were expected to have long hair to demonstrate their connection to the body, to sexuality, and to femininity. Thecla is no longer willing to perform her gender. She wants to cut her hair short like a man's and fulfill her calling as a minister.

Paul is not convinced, though, that Thecla is ready or that the world is ready for her. He replies, "It is a shameful time and you are fair" (25:4).[13] He's worried about what will happen to an unmarried, unprotected young woman who is considered attractive and is now without the relative safety an identity like "wife" and "daughter" would have provided her. Paul's parade-rain continues. He's not only worried about the fact that Thecla is "fair" and might find herself in horrible situations because of other men wanting her; he's also worried that Thecla won't be able to face the next trial, that she won't be able to "stand firm" but will end up being cowardly instead.

Paul here is like that quasi-supportive family member or friend that offers their "support" in the form of fearing the worst and doubting that things can work out for us in the end. Thecla persists, though, and tells Paul, "Only give me the seal of Christ and no trial will touch me" (25:5).[14] She's ready to be baptized. She knows that Christ is all she needs. She has already proven to herself that she can walk through the disappointment, the fear, the heartbreak her choice has caused others, and she can walk through the harm others want to do to her for breaking the rules that they themselves have agreed to follow. She has chosen a new life. She knows this; she has experienced it. She has become someone who hasn't existed before. Someone who is no longer foremost a girl in the eyes of the world but a soul who has chosen her own path.

Paul tells her, though, "Have patience, and you will receive the water" (25:6).[15] He's not convinced that she's ready, or he fears what will happen to her, and consequently to him, if Thecla is baptized and empowered to teach about Christ. Paul's not ready. Whether Thecla is actually qualified enough at this point seems to be less important than the fact that he's just not prepared to have an equal teaching alongside him. He doesn't say no. He says not yet.

But maybe Paul's delay is a grand design at work, and not primarily a prejudice he feels toward her because she's female. Maybe he needs to tell her "not yet" at this point so that something greater can happen next.

THE SIXTH STAGE

That inner treasure must be well-kept, held, and used wisely. This is the sixth stage. It's when we learn to own the hard-won power we've become. It's when we learn to take care of the self we have freed from the circumstances of our birth, from the world around us that wanted us to become someone else, the world that wanted us to be defined by what has already existed.

And what we learn in this sixth stage is how to be our own. We learn to be a self that has never existed before. We learn simply to be true most and only to what we hear within. Because we've completed this journey, because we've understood that all along, ultimately, no matter how far we traveled, the real journey took place from within.

19.

Sacred Rage

And the women were panic-stricken and cried out before the court... "Unholy judgment!"

—*The Acts of Paul and Thecla* 27:2

A fter Paul tells Thecla to be patient when she asks him to baptize her, and then also proceeds to question her courage in the face of another possible trial, he sends Onesiphorus and his family back to Iconium, then travels to Antioch with Thecla. As they enter the city, a very powerful man, described in the scripture as the president of the provincial council of Syria, named Alexander, sees Thecla and becomes obsessed with her. Alexander offers Paul money and gifts in order to take Thecla, but Paul says, "I do not know the woman of whom you speak, nor is she mine" (26:3).[1]

Paul's response is both infuriating and intriguing. It's infuriating because Paul immediately disowns Thecla. He actually pretends he doesn't know her. After all they have been through, when the heat Thecla faces as an unmarried female follower of Christ gets close to Paul, he throws his hands up and severs himself from her and any trouble she might be about to get into. He bails. Paul bails on Thecla, right in this moment when she needs him most. For a second time in Thecla's story, she is called to save herself.

What's intriguing about Paul's response is the significant statement he says at the end of it, "nor is she mine." Women were considered property in Thecla's lifetime, so for Paul to state unequivocally that she is not his reflects the more radical beliefs of their community. Thecla is not his because she's not any man's; she's not his because she can't be owned.

Alexander, "having a lot of power," goes ahead anyway and grabs Thecla on the street. His entitlement rests in his external position of power as a man and as a political leader in Syria. He knows that there are no laws that will protect Thecla, because women were not allowed to be a part of making a single one of them. He knows that there are many laws that will protect his grievous idea that he has a right to take Thecla without her consent.

What Alexander does not realize is that Thecla is no ordinary human being. She has died three days and walked from out of fire unscathed. She has endured the death of her family's love, and the death of her fiancé wishing her harm and turning her in to the authorities. She has endured the horror of her own mother demanding for her to be burned alive, and she has endured the loss of her childhood friends placing the wood on the fire meant to take her life. Thecla is not supported by those around her. Thecla is supported by a love that comes from within her. And she has learned to rely on that inner support (which comes from much more than her alone).

And she knows now that she can trust it. She can trust it, because it's not separate from her. And she has learned to love that source of love, god, that's within her, and to meld with it so completely that to harm her is to harm all that god desires through her.

Thecla knows that she has an innate right to fight to save herself. Thecla knows that love is with her as she fights. Because love is there with us when no one and nothing else is; love is there with us as we do all we can to save the only life we can save.

So when Alexander grabs Thecla right there on the street, the scripture reads, "she would not endure it." Thecla turns to Paul and cries out bitterly, "Do not violate the stranger!" (26:4–5).[2] Then she declares, "I am important among the Iconians" (26:6).[3] This "I am" statement made my blood feel as though it went from flat to carbonated the first time I read it. I am important, Thecla cries out—I am important among the people, my people who tried to kill me, like the voice in *The Thunder, Perfect Mind:* "I am she who is disgraced and she who is important."[4]

Thecla's hometown tried to kill her because she was dangerous to the sexist cultural ideals imposed on women. Her mother declared her a "mad person," for daring to live a life that she herself had never imagined possible. Thecla in this moment, though, flips the script. Or she sees through everything in the searing clarity rage can bring; she's important, and that's why they tried to kill her. She's unlike the women who came before her. She's setting a new example of what might be possible. Thecla is important because she is proof that the powerless can ascend to power. Thecla is proof that we can redirect the source of what guides our choices in life; we can live a life that's ordained from within.

Then Thecla does the unimaginable, in the context of the first century—she demonstrates that she not only knows her inherent worth, she will also claim her responsibility in defending it: "And taking hold of Alexander, she tore off his cloak and took the crown from his head and caused him public shame" (26:7).[5] Thecla physically protects herself from harm. And she's able to do this, to align her words and her actions, with protecting that inner treasure, that love she *knows*—as in, directly experiences from within her—because she has claimed her worth.

Thecla is demonstrating for us that no one is coming to save us—no one except the one we become by saving ourselves.

Of the three possible responses to immediate physical harm—fight, flee, or freeze—I am a freezer. I drop like a possum and play dead. I am the least useful person to have with you in a moment of crisis. I would be the first to go in a zombie apocalypse. I will be stiff as a board and unable to speak. Zero synapses firing. Zero sense of self-preservation. And for a long, long time I was hard on myself for being a freezer rather than a fighter, or even a fleer. I'd take fleeing over freezing any day. I've come to understand, though, and love even, that I am still saving myself through that response. Freezing is an effective way of checking out before pain hits. So I protect myself from the actual conscious experience of physical harm by disassociating from the body before it happens. Like the lithe impala when in the throes of a lion attack. I've learned to love that reptilian part of my brain, that impala-part that I am. Any form of protecting our true self in the face of someone or something that is trying to harm us is an act of resistance.

Thecla is my personal hero, but if you, like me, have never managed to immediately switch into Krav Maga mode the moment you're groped on the subway, just know the rage that surfaces at the boundary that was crossed, the rage that surfaces when you encounter someone acting from their Ignorance and their blindness from the power of Forgetting, the rage that surfaces within you is proof of love's presence. There's a universe of love within you, and glorious rage flares loudly when someone behaves as if the body is flesh only and not also a portal.

This "trial," as Paul refers to it, is about standing up for the self that Thecla has reclaimed. It's about owning the power she is acutely aware resides nowhere else more fully than inside her.

In retaliation, Alexander brings Thecla before the governor. Because Thecla has shamed him by rejecting him, and because if he can't have her, then no one will. The governor sentences Thecla to death by wild beasts in the arena. But unlike her previous trial, when only love is her witness, when only Christ in Paul's form comes to be there with her through the death of who she was before, this time, Thecla is also supported by those around her. She is supported by the love within her and also the people in the crowd who witness Thecla's sentencing as entirely unjust. Specifically, the women in the crowd. The scripture reads, "And the women were panic-stricken and cried out before the court . . . 'Unholy judgment!'" (27:2).[6]

What Thecla acted on in her first trial—a belief in her own worth, a strength of conviction in her own heart, a righteous indignation to live her life according to her own soul and not someone else's ego, is now in her second trial also being supported from outside of her.

This reminds me of a cryptic yet insightful passage from *The Thunder: Perfect Mind:* "What is your inside is your outside . . . and what you see on the outside, you see revealed on the inside."[7] Thecla is not alone anymore, either within herself or externally. There are women in the crowd who see and understand that what happened to Thecla could have, or has, happened to them. They see it as unjust that Thecla is being sentenced to death simply for saying no to a powerful man. Rejection does not warrant death. Rejection may feel like a death to the ego of a powerful man, but it does not justify the actual physical death of the one who refused him.

In Thecla's wisdom of knowing how best to provide for herself even in the worst possible situation, she asks to be given a safe place to stay until her fight with the wild beasts. Similar to Joan of Arc asking to be allowed to keep on her chain mail in prison during her trial to protect her from being assaulted, Thecla asks to be housed where she will not be harmed before her sentence is carried out. So, the scripture relates, "a rich queen, named Tryphaena, whose daughter had died, took Thecla into her care and found solace in her" (27:4).[8]

In Thecla's gown-tearing and de-crowning of Alexander, in her actions to save herself from being harmed, she is recognized by the women around her and finds allies with them. And in her demand to be given sanctuary before her sentence is carried out, she's introduced to a second mother, more worthy of her than the first. In knowing her worth, and in acting in alignment with it, Thecla is given in many ways the healed mother, the mother she always deserved. A woman who reflects now the inner mother Thecla has become to herself.

What's fascinating about the sequence of events in this stage of Thecla's story is that she uses her rage in service of her soul, in order to protect her body. She uses her righteous indignation over the fact that Alexander acted as if he had a right to her body, and her life, and so she tears his crown from off his head. She dethrones him with her rage. This consequently means a second sentencing of death for Thecla, another trial she must face. But also, it means a fierce alignment with greater and more abundant support in the form of the queen, Tryphaena, who represents both a wealth of material resources and a fathomless vat of something Thecla has never received from a woman: unconditional love.

Thecla protects with both her voice and actions the inner treasure she knows exists within her, the treasure she knows makes her life inestimable in the eyes of men.

In an effort to be perceived as good, we have denied ourselves the potency of what rage can empower. There has been considerable cultural and religious conditioning, especially for women and girls, to be "good," which can translate as submissive, silent, controlled. Good, though, is what we are; it's primarily a noun, not an adjective.

Christ explains the human condition in *The Gospel of Mary* by saying, "The Good came into your midst, coming to the good which belongs to every nature" (3:1–6).[9] "The Good" is the non-gendered way the divine is named in Mary's gospel. And the Greek word for "belong" means "to pertain to," and "to reside in." The good then pertains to all of us, and the good resides within us, not once we've reached some elusive ideal of what it might mean to be "good" according to someone outside of us, or according to our own usually intense standards we place on ourselves. That we are good is unconditional.

The good belongs to every nature, which is to say that the good here isn't earned. The good belongs to us. The good is inherent in what it means to be human. It's not performative; we don't have to follow rules created by others, by our family even, about what we have to do to be considered "good."

Good does not mean obedient. Good does not mean doing what we are told to do. Good does not mean controlled by someone else's expectations of us.

Good refers to the nature, the root, the core of who we are. And if we let it, the fact that we are inherently good—that truth alone—can transform us.

We can let go of the guilt, the shame, the feeling of not being enough or of being far too much. We can let go of the idea that we are somehow less, or worth less, because we are human—or because we're not yet "good enough." We can let go of this constant struggle to be perceived as good, or to prove our goodness to others.

Rage and goodness are not mutually exclusive. Rage is often necessary in order to draw fierce boundaries when we or those we love or those we feel connected to are being harmed. And rage is necessary to remind us of our innate goodness. We're angry because we are good, because we recognize, we *know* innately, what is good.

Rage, like a slow controlled burn, can fuel and inform us. Rage can clarify. When we are enraged as the women in the crowd are enraged at seeing Thecla sentenced to death for protecting herself from harm, for simply declaring to Alexander that she is not on offer for him to take, for simply expressing her desire to remain her own, we are experiencing the truth that we are all connected. When the women in the crowd use their rage to give voice to the injustice, to be witnesses to it, Thecla knows she's no longer alone. And this is what makes rage sacred.

When Christine Blasey Ford stood up before the Senate Judiciary Committee in the fall of 2018 during Brett Kavanaugh's confirmation hearing to testify that she had been assaulted by him, I listened to her, and I also listened to the symphony of emotions that coursed through my bloodstream. When Anita Hill was questioned by an all-white, all-male Senate Judiciary Committee in 1991 during her testimony of ongoing sexual harassment by Supreme Court nominee Clarence Thomas, multitudes of women watching saw themselves in her. This was the first time a woman had shared on national television about workplace harassment. And the women watching Anita Hill, like the women watching Christine Blasey Ford, identified with not only the way they had been harassed and assaulted, but also with how their testimony was subsequently discounted, discredited, and ultimately ignored.

The year after Anita Hill testified, a record number of female politicians were elected to office. In Ford's recent memoir, *One Way Back,* she opens with a dedication to all the "letter writers," the tens of thousands who made certain that Ford knows her voice matters. What I felt in both of their testimonies is the way truth reverberates in my body. It's a more ancient frequency; it extends back to the first century, to when a powerful man thought he had the right to assault a woman with immunity, but the women in the crowd all cried out, "Unholy judgment!"

Rage is information. Rage is not an action plan. Rage holds no answers for what's next. And it can quickly galvanize action. Yet, if we act only from that rage, if we move the way rage wants us to move, we will cause harm to ourselves and others. So when we go to take action, we must first intentionally return to love. Rage informs us about what we love, and love moves us to act in ways only love knows.

Rage is my beloved right now.

Glorious rage, red and golden. The rage where everything is broken and everything is sacred. The rage that's entirely my own, the rage that no one else will ever see the inside of or ever fully know. The rage that's sourced from these tremendous wells of unspent love for myself.

The rage that reconfigures what I want for my life. The rage that grabs my face and forces me to see that I haven't loved yet someone who wants more for me than I know how to want for myself. The rage that tears everything down inside me, tears everything up, too, all the contracts written, all the cords and threads ever tied to anyone who doesn't actually see me. The rage that keeps my heart soft, and my boundaries unbroken. The rage that comes from the single most significant truth: I only have so much time here.

The rage that makes certain I find that love of my life, I write that sentence that's coiled at the base of my spine, I kiss that kiss that reaches through to the soul. The rage that has only ever been meant for me, to move me to the most powerful place in existence, which is the joy I alone can live from, the joy I alone can share.

The rage that love inspires, the rage that still calls out from the crowd, breaking the spell of what's expected. The rage that reminds us we can take up space. We can know our own worth. We can live with the fierce clarity purpose gives. We can be as brilliant as we really are and never spend our energy ever again on hiding it. We can know how important we are, how our one life constellates a universe of potential. And we can love in a way where we don't need anyone else to love us in order for it to seemingly seep from us, as if we're actually filled with it, brimming with it, as if love itself is seeping out from within us, from the marrow of our bones.

20.

Sacrilege

And the women along with the children cried out from above,
saying, "God, a godless judgment has been passed in this city!"

—*The Acts of Paul and Thecla* 28:3

The Roman soldiers bind Thecla to a lioness and place a placard around her neck that states the charge of her crime: "Sacrilege." Sacrilege is the word that Thecla has to wear while tethered to a lioness and paraded through the streets alongside the wild animals that will be poked and prodded in order to attack her in the arena the next day.

The queen stays close, and follows behind Thecla to make sure Thecla knows she isn't alone. Out of curiosity, people begin to line the streets and watch from open windows above as the morbid parade passes raucously down below. Rather than a great danger or threat, though, the lioness that Thecla is bound to suddenly stops and sits down in front of her. And to everyone's amazement, the lioness begins to lick Thecla's feet, as if now devoted to her. As soon as this happens, "the women along with the children cried out from above, saying, 'God, a godless judgment has been passed in this city'" (28:3).[1]

After the procession, the queen invites Thecla to stay with her again for the night. Her daughter, Falconilla, who recently passed away, visited her in a dream that prepared the queen for Thecla's arrival. Falconilla told the queen in the dream, "You will have the lonely stranger, Thecla, in place of me so that she might pray for me and I might be transferred to the place of the just" (28:4).[2] So, on the second night that the queen gives Thecla sanctuary, she says, "Thecla, my second child, come here and pray for my child so that she might live forever, for I saw this in a dream" (29:1).[3]

At the queen's request, Thecla, without hesitation, lifts her voice and says, "My God, the child of the Highest, the One in heaven, give her according to her wish so that her daughter, Falconilla, might live forever" (29:2).[4] After hearing Thecla's prayer for her daughter, the queen mourns the fact that Thecla will have to fight the wild animals the next day. She loves Thecla as fiercely as she had loved her own daughter.

At dawn, Alexander arrives to take Thecla from the queen—since he is the one who had offered the "games," which is how he refers to the death sentence that has been passed on Thecla. Alexander says, "The governor is seated and the crowd is clamoring for us. Take away she who is to fight the wild animals" (30:1).[5]

But Tryphaena cries out, "A second mourning for my Falconilla has come upon my house and there is no one to help—neither my child, for she is dead, nor relatives, for I am a widow" (30:2).[6] The queen's rage mixed with anguish and raw emotion scares Alexander, so he leaves without taking Thecla.

Thecla has now been fully claimed by the queen; she exclaims, "God of my child Thecla, help Thecla!" (30:3).[7]

The definition of the word "sacrilege" is "stealer of sacred things." A sacrilege is a violation, a misuse of what is commonly regarded as sacred.

What is it that we hold sacred? What is the real sacrilege here? Thecla's second refusal to become someone's property? Or the fact that Alexander tries with his brute force to take Thecla as his own against her will?

When I was held down against my will, it fundamentally changed my relationship to the word "surrender." And it fundamentally transformed my relationship to the word "power."

For me, a consciousness arrived when someone else's physical strength decided what happened to my body. It served as a pinpoint of light during the absolutely most barren, and terrifying, moment. I won't fall back on clichés like "the resilience of the human spirit." It feels crucial to name this consciousness more precisely. Because it's invisible, and intangible, and yet it's far more powerful than any physical strength could exact upon me. It comes from within. And it met me there, in that most bleak and irredeemable moment. It was powerless compared to the physical strength that was overpowering my will for myself; it's powerless to stop what might happen to us. And yet, it's a strength so tremendous that human muscle is an imitation of it; the human strength of one person is a minuscule fraction of the might it possesses.

It's an essence that's enduring. It's soft, and quiet, and so pervasive it would be too limiting to say it has to do with the heart, or the soul, or the spirit within each of us. Because it's also more than us. Here's the difference between the brute force of physical human muscle and the limitless power of what some of us who have been held down against our will have encountered—the brute force comes from one human person, one human body, one human ego, one human life. The limitless power that resides within us is a power that connects us to everyone who has ever suffered, everyone who has ever known pain, every loved one including those who have passed away who loved us completely; it's a power derived from everyone who has ever wanted love and joy for our lives and not this pain.

I was not alone. My body will never forget both the powerlessness and the power that met me from within. This power that was with me all along. This power that connects me to a countless many. It's the only place I can bear to use the word "surrender," the only place where it actually feels appropriate, and sacred. To surrender inward to this power that's within.

Symbolically, the lion represents spiritual courage. In a Christian context, specifically, the lion represents the might and power of Christ. And a lioness in particular is a reference to protection. What's even more significant within the context of the Roman Empire is that the most coveted male virtue was courage. Scholars of the early Christ Movement explain, "Courage is actually synonymous with manliness in this context; the Greek word courage, *andreia,* is formed from a root meaning 'man' (andr). Courage, therefore, is equivalent to 'being a man.' "[8]

For Thecla's story to be so directly associated then to this well-recognized symbol of courage itself challenged the cultural norms of the ancient Mediterranean, where only the male body was considered a fully formed human being. As scholars of the early Christ Movement relate, "Gender is obviously, then, a hugely important tool, perhaps the most important tool, as a person or group explores and defines identity."[9]

So let's see this scene again of Thecla being paraded through the streets tethered to a lioness.

Thecla refuses to let Alexander assault her on the street; she screams out in protest, and tears his crown from his head. Alexander—as if he is the one who has been wronged—provides the "games" for Thecla to be sentenced to death in the arena by wild animals. Thecla—as punishment for shaming Alexander by refusing him—is paraded through the street wearing the word "sacrilege" while tethered to a lioness. The curious gather to watch, and maybe some jeer, maybe some feel excited for the "entertainment" she'll soon provide. But the women and children scream out the truth that what's happening is "godless," that a "godless judgment has been passed."

Thecla can hear and feel that she's not alone. She's surrounded by the voice of support and understanding. She has a companion in her second mom, the queen walking alongside her. And she's tethered from the start to a lioness or to the spiritual courage and protection that will help her survive this second trial. The symbol of the most coveted masculine virtue is physically connected to her, reminding her that she is not now and has never been less than any other simply for being female.

Thecla is wearing the word "sacrilege" because she dared to call out a man for abusing her. She was unafraid of his political power. And yet the women and children reflect that the true sacrilege is sentencing Thecla to face the wild animals. It's a sacrilege to obey the laws that allow Thecla to be treated like property, and then to punish her for not being controlled, for refusing him. It's a sacrilege to support Alexander in his gaslighting stance that he's the one who has been harmed. It's a sacrilege to support those who exert their physical power, and their own will over the spiritual will of any person. This is the true sacrilege, in the first century as much as it is in the twenty-first—suggesting that Thecla doesn't own or know her own body and doesn't get to live the life she wills for herself.

21

Authority

"In the name of Jesus Christ, I baptize myself."

—The Acts of Paul and Thecla 34:3

A fter Alexander fails to bring Thecla to the arena, the governor sends soldiers to Tryphaena's home to take her by force. And although Tryphaena can't stop the soldiers from taking Thecla, she refuses to leave her side. The queen takes hold of Thecla's hand, so that they can walk toward the arena together. She explains, "I brought my daughter, Falconilla, to the grave, and you, Thecla, I bring to fight the wild animals" (31:2).[1]

Then Thecla cries ferociously and yells out, "Lord God in whom I trust, with whom I have taken refuge, who rescued me from the fire, render reward to Tryphaena" (31:3).[2] There is an uproar and rumbling of wild animals as if in response to Thecla's prayer. The crowd shouts out as the soldiers lead

Thecla and the queen into the arena, "some saying, 'Bring in the sacrilegious one!' but others saying, 'Let the city be destroyed for this lawlessness!'" (32:1).[3]

Thecla and Tryphaena's clasped hands are forced apart by the soldiers. Then Thecla is stripped (again with the stripping). She is given only an undergarment to wear, and then she's led farther into the arena. The lions and bears are released and begin to pace in front of her. A lioness charges at Thecla, but instead of attacking her, the lioness lies down in front of her—guarding her (33:3).[4] The scripture doesn't specify if it's the same lioness who had stopped in the procession the day before to lick Thecla's feet. But the symbolism of Christ's protection and of the spiritual courage she possesses are radiantly clear as she stands in the center of the arena.

When a wild bear charges at Thecla, the lioness runs out to meet the bear and tears the bear apart. Then a lion, which had been trained by Alexander to kill humans, charges at Thecla. The fierce lioness goes out again to protect her, and dies in the process of killing the lion for the sake of Thecla's survival. Then the scripture says that the women in the crowd mourn more than ever because the lioness that had been helping Thecla is now dead.

Just as the soldiers release more wild animals into the arena, Thecla stands up and stretches her hands out to pray. As she finishes the prayer, she turns toward a great pit of water in the center of the arena that contains sea lions. As Thecla immerses herself in the water, she declares for everyone to hear, "In the name of Jesus Christ I baptize myself" (34:3).[5]

While watching this unfold, the crowd pleads with Thecla not to throw herself into the water, fearing that the sea lions are going "to devour such beauty" (34:4). The scripture describes that even the governor wept. But as Thecla enters the water, there's a great flash of light, and all the sea lions float to the surface. And Thecla is suddenly, miraculously surrounded by a cloud of fire so that she's both shielded from the wild animals and also from being seen naked by the spectators. A second miracle in Thecla's story arrives right after she baptizes herself.

The Pulitzer Prize–winning novelist Toni Morrison writes in her masterpiece *Beloved,* "Freeing yourself was one thing, claiming ownership of that freed self was another."

How do we learn to trust the voice we can only hear from within?

Authority starts with integrity. It's about learning to hear, inwardly, the truth of what we already know is right for us and then claiming ownership of it by giving voice to it.

What's so electrifying about this moment in Thecla's story is that no one gives her permission to baptize herself. The authority comes from within her. Thecla acts with absolute integrity. She prays, which to me is a return to the heart, a return to the source of what's true for her. And then she notices the pool of water, and aligns with what she had been wanting since she survived the first trial: to be baptized. But this time, she doesn't ask anyone outside of her for permission or guidance. She is led from within—connected as she is to the truth of love, the love that has been leading her since she first heard the word "beloved" in Paul's teachings.

The theological paradigm within the Christian tradition since the fourth century has operated as a hierarchy. God is understood to be cast far above humanity and outside of what it means to be human. God is the ultimate power. God is masculine, a father, and in a position of absolute authority. God within this theological paradigm replicates and divinely affirms the social structure of a patriarchy. And whether someone is

Christian or not, the patriarchy is pervasive. The concept of an ultimate authority existing outside of us is as much a social construct as it is a theological one.

Why is there so much misuse of power reported and covered up within the church? Because this theological paradigm of an ultimate authority existing outside of us is a breeding ground for it. It asks us to suspend what we might know, what we are hearing from within us, loud and clear, about an actual human being in a robe, or in a position of spiritual authority within the church.

This paradigm asks us to hand over our own personal power and to see someone else as more than we are, and even sometimes more than human. It asks us to assign ourselves, and the voice within us, to be less consequential than the voice that's behind the pulpit. It asks us to displace what we know to be true or right, in order to follow the dictates of this ordained person. It asks us to trust another more than we trust ourselves. It asks us to think that god exists only on a vertical axis, way up at the top, and looks down on us, deigns to be with us, and so our position is subservient. And that same position is then replicated within the church hierarchy. We are subservient to those ordained to be the voice of god.

This paradigm, though, of a god that only exists outside of us, above and beyond us, actually goes against the belief systems of Christianity. Even within the most conservative churches, god is understood and believed to be omniscient, omnipotent, omnibenevolent, and omnipresent. With these four "omnis," god is everywhere, knows everything, and is an equally powerful force of good within all things.

Constantine consecrated the patriarchy as a divine constellation of god's being, an idea that ensured his own power. The patriarchy, however, is a human construct. And maybe it has run its course; maybe we're beginning to see that the patriarchy has actually never served humanity.

More importantly, the patriarchy has never actually done justice to the most foundational theological ideas about god. It has never and can never reflect the ultimate ineffable power, knowing, goodness, and presence of god, which is love.

What if the paradigm for understanding god shifts so that god remains ultimate and above us, beyond us, beyond what our human minds can ever fully comprehend—and then also, what if we accept that god is within? What if god is also a goodness within all things, and a love that knows itself completely?

Then we can listen to those in positions of spiritual authority, *and*—this is the most critical difference—we can also know and acknowledge that the voice of love exists within. We can listen to an authority outside of us while also refusing to silence the voice of knowing within us.

It's not so much a decentralizing of power and authority in the church as it as a *remembering* of the fact that there were those in the earliest recorded teachings after the crucifixion who believed and practiced that yes, there are spiritual leaders, and also, there's a basilica, a royal power within each one of us as well.

When I finally met Jacob from the bible in real life, it confirmed everything I had already felt in his words. Fruits of justice radiated out of his pores like infinitesimal moonbeams. He's impossibly tall and thin, like a stick of well-dressed dynamite. We were in Rhinebeck, New York, at a spiritual retreat center called the Omega Institute. I had invited him as a guest to attend the Mary Magdalene Revealed Retreat, and he offered to sing. What I didn't realize until I saw him perform live for the first time is that music is his ministry. He tossed out pearls to us in the audience during his "small talk" between songs, like, "My favorite emotion is surprise. Because if you're surprised, it means your world has changed."

During a Q and A on the last day, a small-in-stature-fierce-in-energy-type lady walked up to the mic. I loved her before she started talking. Her name in Hebrew means "praised," and Praised told us about how effortless it had always been for her to love the people in her life. She drenched them in love. Irrational, unconditional, and unspeakable amounts of it. What she could see now, though, was that she rarely feels that love reciprocated. She would get crumbs in comparison to what she doled out in handfuls. During the meditation we had just practiced together, she realized something transformational. She heard something real and true for her. Something that both scared and excited her, because she had been changed by it. Then Praised paused, took a deep, deliberate intake of air, lionized her heart, and said with this triumphant flair I'll never forget, "Crumbs are no longer delicious!"

I could see that Praised heard my "hallelujah" amidst the raucous sound of the entire auditorium rushing to their feet to cheer for her. I was in tears from locking eyes with her. And I wanted that T-shirt, in a bold font, straight across my chest.

Hundreds of us came together from around the world out of our shared curiosity about the scriptures that were left out of the New Testament in the fourth century. And to practice what it's like to meditate together, so we can *know* love, as from the Greek, *gnosis*, meaning knowledge gained from direct experience.

Christ says in *The Gospel of Mary*, "Beware that no one lead you astray saying, 'Look over here!' Or 'Look over there!' For the Child of Humanity is within you!" (4:3–5).[6] The Child of Humanity, sometimes translated as "the true human being," is the *anthropos*. It's someone who practices uniting the self with the soul, to see less with the ego and more with the eye of the heart. It's not a permanent condition; oh, how I wish that were the case. It's a perpetual effort, a momentary grace; when, after years of inner work, love breaks through within us to where it has never reached before. Mercy takes up residence within us in a way that we are indelibly changed.

Salvation in its original context meant simply "to be made more alive." This is what we practice in essence; we practice saving ourselves in this way, together, like Thecla. We practice together the authority she claimed to be made more alive.

22.

Freedom

And the governor called out to Thecla from the midst of the
wild animals and said to her, "Who are you? And what is it
about you that not even one of the wild animals touched you?"

—*The Acts of Paul and Thecla* 37:1–2

Thecla embodies true power. By baptizing herself, Thecla reveals to the entire arena that she is the ultimate authority of her own life. And suddenly, it's as if the women in the crowd recognize her; they recognize the fruits of justice in her face. They witness her baptism, her third act of saving herself in her story, and their voices of dissent are no longer enough. Now they must also act on her behalf. They feel compelled to replicate the integrity they see in Thecla. They have to align what's within them with action. They're no longer separate from her. What's happening to Thecla is understood now as a collective injustice.

The women know that this has never just been about Thecla. This has always been about freedom. The freedom to choose the life we're meant to live when we're being guided from within. And so, the women in the crowd stop being spectators and participants in her sentencing. This is the moment they choose to work together with Thecla in her freedom. They begin to act in ways they never have before; they are freed to join Thecla in her fight to save herself.

As other, even more frightening, wild animals are released into the arena, the women "cried aloud, and some threw petals, while others nard, and others cinnamon, and yet others cardamom, so that there was an abundance of perfumes. And all the wild animals which were let out were held as if by sleep and did not touch her" (35:1–2).[1]

Alexander takes this moment to brag to the governor, "I have exceedingly terrorizing bulls," and suggests that they bind the bulls to "the one who is to fight the wild animals" (35:2). The governor, who looks sad now, according to the scripture, answers, "Do what you will" (35:3). The guards bind Thecla by the feet between two bulls. Then they place burning irons on the bulls' genitals in order to enrage them, so that as they race off in opposite directions, they will kill Thecla in the process. But just as the rope is pulled taut between Thecla and the bulls, "a consuming flame burned through the ropes and Thecla was as if she had not been bound" (35:5).[2] This is the third miracle in her story, one that arrives right after the women in the crowd join Thecla in her effort of saving herself.

The queen's poor body finally gives out; Thecla has had one too many near-death experiences for her nervous system to manage. She passes out so impressively on the stage near the governor that she's mistaken as dead. At the sight of the queen sprawled out before him, a strike of fear threads its way through Alexander. Because he realizes suddenly that he could be harmed. He remembers that the queen is related to the emperor, and if he finds out the queen died from the trauma and terror of watching Thecla be tormented and killed by him, then the governor, himself, and the city will all be destroyed.

Alexander immediately approaches the governor, falls to his knees, and pleads, "Have mercy on both me and the city and acquit the animal fighter in case the city be destroyed with her" (36:2).[3] So the governor then calls out to Thecla, who is still standing in the middle of the arena, and asks her, "Who are you? And what is it about you that not even one of the wild animals touched you?" (37:2).[4]

What is freedom but the ability to answer this question: "Who are you?" And what is freedom but the capacity to then live out the answer?

Thecla says, "I indeed am the slave of the living God. And as to what it is about me, I have trusted in the Child of God, in whom he finds pleasure, and through whom not even one of the wild animals touched me. For this one alone is the limit of salvation and the foundation of life through the ages . . . a refuge for those in a storm; freedom for the oppressed; for the despairing a shelter" (37:3–4).[5]

According to scholars of the first hundred years of the Christ Movement, "In The Acts of Paul and Thecla, apparently the young woman leader Thecla (and perhaps Paul) belong to a group that is called 'the Enslaved of God.'"[6] In Thecla's time, there was an empire-wide program of enslavement with every Roman military conquest—"Roman soldiers captured thousands of inhabitants of the subjugated territories and enslaved them to serve the empire's ever-expanding domination."[7] For a group within the Christ Movement to refer to themselves as the Enslaved of God would be to directly challenge the Roman Empire's enslavement of them. With this name, they are suggesting that, first, their true "ruler" is not the emperor. And second, even more transgressively, that their "ruler," this god they're enslaved to, is more powerful than the emperor.

Thecla's statement, "I indeed am the slave of the living God," is perhaps evidence that she was a part of the community within the Christ Movement called the Enslaved of God. Some of the other communities that made up the Christ Movement were known as "the Body of the Anointed," "Brothers and Sisters," and simply "the Way."[8]

These communities aimed to model Christ by taking care of one another, no matter how they ranked according to the Roman hierarchy. The various groups of the Christ Movement practiced that gender was fluid and flexible: "One of the primary identities was that they were neither male nor female, but all were 'one' through different lived, experienced realities of gender pluralism."[9] Followers of the Enslaved of God would, like Thecla, express themselves in ways that felt most aligned with who they were from within them. Women cut their hair short, and men grew their hair long. This created new possibilities for what it meant to be "human," rather than the prescribed cultural ideals and expectations placed solely based on sex and gender.

The communities and groups of the early Christ Movement had no form of hierarchical leadership, and according to scholars, they actually had little interest in telling one another how to practice their faith or what to believe. Again, their focus was on feeding one another, literally and metaphorically. They nourished the members of their community. "Supper clubs" became a crucial aspect in their care for one another.[10] The etymology of the word "companion" is formed from the Latin word *com*, meaning "together with," and *panis*, meaning "bread." The

Old French *compaignon* means "one who breaks bread with another." This companionship is at the heart of what it meant to be a part of the Christ Movement.

The size of these groups started at around two thousand people about twenty years after Christ's death, and grew to possibly a total of twenty thousand by fifty years later. Their groups were comprised of mostly peasants, day workers, the enslaved, migrants, and craftspeople.[11] What impacted them most profoundly was being surrounded by people who would treat each other like family. This is why this movement was so radical; they offered one another an alternative to the *paterfamilias,* to the patriarchal structure embedded in Roman culture.

The early Christ Movement rejected the status quo of father-led families. The father-led family, the *paterfamilias,* was a hierarchical relationship modeled after the ultimate "father"—Rome itself, personified by the emperor. So in a very real way, by rejecting their own father-led family structures, these communities were also directly challenging the power of the empire.

Slavery was everywhere throughout Roman society. The Roman Empire in the first century had conquered the nations around the Mediterranean. Military conquests meant enslavement of the inhabitants of subjugated territories. By the mid-second century, half the population of the city of Rome were descendants of enslaved people.

Therefore, Roman violence was a primary concern for the earliest followers of Christ. Violence was strategic. Violence helped ensure that those on the lower rungs of the Roman Empire's social structure, especially those from conquered nations, considered themselves as subhuman. And while the empire brought benefit to some select citizens, the overwhelming majority experienced profound loss, trauma, and dehumanization. So in response to the empire's brutality and oppression, these communities came together to exist as companions, as "true human beings," and as siblings to one another. And they demonstrated that their kindness and love could never be ruled, controlled, or manipulated. They demonstrated their love for one another as an act of resistance.

Belonging to one of these groups from the Christ Movement was a crucial way for the under-heard, the enslaved, the day laborers, and the migrants from across the empire to provide safety and security for one another. There are three Greek words associated with these communities: *synodos,* or company; *synergasia,* or fellow workers; and *synagogue,* or assembly. They all start with *syn,* which is Greek for "with." This "with-ness," scholars argue, is what made these groups so powerful, and so threatening.[12] Because they were not participating in the divisions imposed on them from Roman society. They were refusing to be a part of a structure of power that kept them separate from one another.

They practiced together a power that was *with* them, from within them. They created a space safe from the pervasive impact of a power over them. They practiced relating to one another with love, and existing together as equals. Experiencing together what it was like to be seen, to exist to someone else, even a stranger, in one of these gatherings, not primarily as a woman or a man, as a wife or a husband, as a citizen or a slave, as a wealthy person or a peasant; not as a title or a role that could be ranked, but as human beings. In the midst of pervasive state violence and social brokenness, they offered one another a safe place to be fed, to be seen, and to just exist as they were, whoever that might be.

I can hear the resonance of Praised's revelation here, that

these groups, these "supper clubs" were so threatening because by feeding one another, by refusing to be divided, they were also saying, "Crumbs are no longer delicious." Crumbs of a proximal power no longer suffice. In being together, they regain clarity that in fact they represent the majority.

Maybe all the trials in our lives prepare us to know the answer to this question: "Who are you?"

And freedom is not only being able to express it, but then also to demonstrate it to others, so that we become living proof, and therefore permission, for others to live from the inside out as well.

THE SEVENTH STAGE

And this is the seventh and final stage. It's the return to the place where the call first came from. It's a reintegration of that life before the revelation came. But it's an entirely new person who returns to the start. Or it's the person we already were from the beginning. It's just that now, we have become our own. We are no one else's expectations. We are no one else's possession. We are no longer the fulfillment of what others desire for us to be or become. We are now just the truth of who we are.

We have pulled back, and reclaimed all the power we had been projecting onto the people and the places we called home. We have returned home, or we are now finally home for the first time, because all of that power is realized as something that had always been within us, sitting there silently, as if behind a small door, a hidden reliquary in the back of our back. The place we couldn't reach before because we didn't know it existed yet, because we didn't yet exist fully within ourselves.

23.

The Women All Cried Out
in a Loud Voice

And the women all cried out in a loud voice, as if from one
mouth, and gave praise to God, saying, "One is God who has
saved Thecla!" so that the whole city shook from their voice.

—The Acts of Paul and Thecla 38:5

The governor orders for clothes to be brought to
Thecla, and then he says to her, "Put on these garments" (38:1).[1] But as Thecla takes the clothes from
him, she explains, "The one who clothed me when I was naked
among the wild beasts is this one who will clothe me with salvation in the day of judgment" (38:2).[2]

Thecla wants to make sure it's radiantly clear that she is not
putting back on the layers of the ego that she took off when this
all began, when she went to the prison to see Paul for herself,
face-to-face, and offered her bracelets and her silver mirror to the
guards for admission. Thecla is not going backward. She is not
clothing herself again with the trappings of a culture, a system of
power, an empire that does not and cannot possibly define her.

At the end of *The Gospel of Mary,* after Mary has revealed to the disciples (at Peter's request) the secret teachings that Christ intentionally gave to her, Peter doesn't believe her. He practically scoffs, "Has the Savior spoken secretly to a woman and not openly so that we would all hear? Surely, he did not want to show that she is more worthy than we are?" (10:3–4).[3]

Levi comes to Mary's defense, first by calling out Peter's anger management issues. He says, "Peter, you have always been an angry person" (10:7).[4] And then he says something I wish with every thread of who I am the disciples could have heard, and that we all might have the capacity to hear now: "If the Savior considered her to be worthy, who are you to disregard her?" (10:9).[5]

What Peter can't see, what his Rage clouds, is that in giving Mary secret teachings, Christ is demonstrating that she is as worthy as he is, and the other male disciples. She is not less or more. Equal to. Instead of rejecting Mary's teachings, instead of silencing her for millennia and discrediting her gospel, instead of telling lies about her with the invention of "the penitent prostitute," in the hope of derailing her authority, Levi suggests, "We should clothe ourselves with the perfect Human, acquire it for ourselves as he commanded us, and proclaim the good news" (10:11–12).[6]

Essentially, Levi's message is that we can't wear the emperor's clothes; we can't pretend that those titles and labels and ideas of ourselves are true anymore. We can't fit back into what has been shed, transformed. As we return to the world, post-baptism, we don't have to necessarily wear different "clothes," but we have to wear those same clothes differently. Meaning we might put back on, for example, the same roles and titles that we held before, that covered our lives with meaning. Titles of parentage, of our position at work, or the long-established role in the family. It's just that now we know, as in we've experienced directly, that our truest self is not conditional; it does not rely on a relationship outside of us to fulfill it. Our truest self is this self that never changes, this unconditional love that resides within.

We may look externally the exact same. It's just that now we understand that as we exist in this world with all these names and titles and critical roles to play in other people's lives; we also, and foremost, stay anchored to the love that's with us in all that we do.

So we are to clothe ourselves not with how the external world might define us. We are not going to "dress" according to the constructs of who we can and must be according to the systems of power outside of us but rather with "the perfect Human," which is the English translation from the Greek word *anthropos*, meaning "fully human and fully divine."

According to *The Gospel of Mary*, we are to "acquire it for ourselves as he commanded us." And we acquire the *anthropos*, the perfect Human, through the practice of *kenosis*, this art of remembering the truth of love amid what's most human in us. This simple, profound work of turning inward with awareness and bringing all our focus into the heart. So that we are present to what happens to be present for us in that moment. No matter how many of the seven egoic powers are at work concurrently in our lives, we recognize each for what they are: a power of the ego. And with that recognition, that seeing and being seen of our own humanity, we can release it, and allow a power far deeper, and far more ancient and otherworldly, to come flooding back through us and into our lives.

In *The Gospel of Mary*, the soul is non-gendered. Our sex and our sexuality inform but do not preclude our capacity to hold positions of authority. The communities that considered

The Acts of Paul and Thecla and *The Gospel of Mary* sacred scripture in the first several centuries of the Christ Movement understood and practiced that gender is not a determinate factor of leadership. What matters is the depth of spiritual transformation a person is willing to undergo, and continues to practice.

One of the ways that these early communities that comprised the Christ Movement responded to Roman violence with resistance was through the announcement of "good news." The English word translated as "gospel," meaning "good news," was not originally a religious expression. "Gospel" is derived from the Old English word *godspel,* which simply meant a pronouncement of something positive. What's powerful here, though, is that the Latin word it translates, *evangelium,* originally referred to statements made by the Roman Empire when yet another conquest was made. Proclamations of an ever-expanding empire would be constant reminders of the pervasive violence and trauma for those with little to no power within it.

So instead, members of the Christ Movement had their own good news. It included seemingly inconsequential moments, compared to the empire's conquests, like a healing or a harvest: "This good news was not about winning a great battle or gaining a material foothold. Nor was it about gaining assurance of life in the afterlife. What made a difference for these communities was caring for one another, bestowing forgiveness, being fed, finding a future, and being surrounded by companions."[7]

After the governor hands Thecla some clothes, and after Thecla makes clear that she'll never wear the empire's clothes again (but that she'll kindly take the clothes he gives her so she's no longer naked), the governor announces to Thecla and to the entire arena, "I release you" (38:4).[8]

What happens next is arguably the crowning moment of her entire story. Because all along, Thecla's story was about more than just her own freedom. All along, her story has been a single instrument within a far larger story of what personal freedom can orchestrate. Thecla is the spark, or the lit wick of a single candle that starts a blaze, a wildfire. Thecla is just the start. She's the hope. The possibility. The Good News. The hard-won freedom we each individually can make of our lives. What's next is what's beyond freedom. And it's called joy.

The moment the governor announces to Thecla that she is released, "the women all cried out in a loud voice, as if from one mouth, and gave praise to God, saying, 'One is God who has saved Thecla!' so that the whole city shook from their voice" (38:5).[9]

It's the women in the crowd who refuse to be spectators and participants in her death, and instead defy the empire together, pooling their collective power and resources—the rose petals, the nard, the cardamom—to save Thecla from the injustice she has been sentenced to.

It's the women in the crowd who refuse to see Thecla as separate from them. It's the women in the crowd who refuse to follow the directives of a system of power outside of them ordering them to continue to be a part of its hold over everyone, as if they realize in watching Thecla's struggle to stay alive in the arena that they have all their lives actually been lulled into a form of stupor themselves by the promises of proximal power, siphoned to them through their husbands and fathers.

And now, because the injustice of Thecla's death sentence in the arena is so compelling, the rage of it wakes them, fully, and they see the cracks in the hold the empire has over them. They see that actually one of them can be murdered, one at a time, but all of them cannot be killed all at once. One of them can be silenced, when a powerful man tries to assault her in the street, and accuses her of being a sacrilege simply for defending herself from harm. One of them can have her voice shattered, by living in a world that can't see her worth. But they see now, they experience directly, that if they unify, if they work together, "in a loud voice, as if from one mouth," they can save each other, every single one of them.

There's a timeless formula found here in this scripture: No amount of powerlessness is without power once unified.

Tryphaena, the queen, "receiving the good news," comes to meet Thecla in the crowd and embraces her. I can see this moment like a scene in a movie—the camera zooms in on the two that had been unjustly torn from each other, and now we see them up close, just as they are reunited, triumphant. And it's both literal and archetypal, both an actual moment in time between two historical figures, when the heroine has won, and a symbolic moment when the feminine within the patriarchy is finally healed, restored. When the bond between women, and the bond between mother and daughter, is no longer confined and burdened by the need to compete for scraps of power, or for a mother to conform and distort her daughter into someone she or they are not. When the bond between mother and daughter is freed from the weight of sacrifice for the sake of pleasing others, to perpetuate the costly ideal of the "good girl."

Thecla here in this moment, in being embraced by unconditional love, represents the power of providing for herself what she had never received before. She has met with, by becoming herself, the mother freed from the patriarchy.

Tryphaena says, "'Now I trust that my child lives! Come inside, and I will assign to you all the things that are mine.' Then Thecla went in with her and rested in her house for eight days, instructing her in the word of God. . . . And there was great joy in the house" (39:2).[10]

This is the absolute opposite moment to when Thecla left her little redbrick house and her life after hearing Paul outside her window. Here in this house, with the queen as her mother, Thecla is free. She can be who she is without confining herself to the life her biological mother expected of her, the life that the outside world of the Roman Empire demanded of her as a girl.

Rather than a mother who offers her own daughter to be burned at the stake for defying the empire, here we have a "queen" mother for Thecla who proclaims, "Now I trust that my child lives!" Truly lives. Here in this house, with the family Thecla has made by becoming her own, by being true to what she heard from within her, Thecla can experience joy. Thecla here is free to choose a life that isn't confined to what has happened before. Thecla is truly alive. Meaning she is guided by the dictates of her own soul. And this second mother is a queen in the sense that symbolically she represents the elusive wealth that only the soul can provide us.

Thecla's story demonstrates to us what becomes possible when we refuse to be divided, when women refuse to abandon themselves and each other, and when a person with little personal agency or political power refuses to let others define them: Joy. This is why we endure all that transformation demands, to find the place where joy is a choice again. More joy than we've ever yet imagined. Embedded in Thecla's story is a promise hidden since antiquity but meant for us now, today——there's a singular joy on the other side of unifying "in a loud voice, as if from one mouth."

24

The Girl Who Baptized Herself

"I have received a bath, Paul. For the one who worked together with you for the good news also worked together with
me in my baptism."

—The Acts of Paul and Thecla 40:4

After Thecla spends time in her new home with the queen, scripture relates that she begins to miss Paul. She soon finds out that he is in Myra, which is in the present-day Antalya Province of Turkey. So, before leaving, "she bound herself up and stitched together her garment—a robe in the fashion of a man's" (40:2).[1]

Thecla travels to Myra with "a crowd" following her. Eventually, she finds Paul. And per usual, he's in the middle of telling stories about Christ, as he was years ago when they first met. So this is when everything has changed, and everything has stayed the same.

Thecla arrives in an outfit she created herself. The fact that Thecla "bound herself up" suggests the sacredness of being freed from the strict gender binaries that existed in the first century and remain in most parts of the modern world. She's wearing a garment she stitched together herself, "a robe in the fashion of a man's." She's presenting as a person who exists outside of the confines of male and female. Thecla is demonstrating to us how sacred it is to be authentic.

I imagine the sight of Thecla, entirely her own, even down to her clothes, shocked Paul. But maybe even more than the fact that Thecla is wearing something similar to what he might have had on, she is surrounded by a crowd of people. And maybe this is what makes him so astonished at the sight of her.

The scripture implies that Paul has a flashback of sorts and thinks at first that Thecla is knee-deep in another trial when he sees the large number of people following her. Realizing his confusion, Thecla clarifies, "I have received a bath, Paul. For the one who worked together with you for the good news also worked together with me in my baptism" (40:4).[2]

There are so many comments Thecla makes in her story that compel me to feel a sense of awe and admiration for her, eliciting a quiet *damn, girl.* This one is so fierce and subtle; it sings of a perfected mastery in letting Paul know, in the most gentle and emotional kung fu way, that the same ultimate power of love, god, the good, who works with him in his ministry is the same god, the same good, who has worked together with Thecla to baptize her. This one statement redirects the power of who can ordain and be ordained back to god. It isn't a set of external circumstances—sex, gender, sexuality—that delimits and determines who can become ministers.

It's ultimately a power that works together through us but doesn't begin or end in any individual one of us. It wasn't up to Thecla that she was called, just as it wasn't up to Paul whether or not she could be baptized and then minister. That power, that love, exists within Thecla, and works together with and through her.

Then Paul takes Thecla's hand and leads her to a house filled with those waiting to hear from him about Christ. And instead, they hear from Thecla. Paul demonstrates here the way he has been transformed because of her; he sits down among the crowd to listen and lets her speak.

We can only imagine what she might have said, but I have to believe that she shared the unique ways she struggled to answer the call to ministry because she is female, the worth she reclaimed to stand face-to-face with Paul, the price she paid at the prison to draw closer to a freedom she had never thought possible, the truth she found by discarding all the trappings of her gender, that look of love that met her as she walked naked through the crowd in her hometown that had disowned her, how love was there for her when no one and nothing else was, how trusting this love led to miracles, being saved by a downpour and later by spontaneous bursts of fire and light, how this love gave her a courage that comes from within her that has the strength of her conviction, how an otherworldly power rose up from within her to be with her as she fought off an assault, how a fierce lioness protected her in the arena against the wild animals that were meant to kill her, and about the singular ways she was saved by women all throughout her ministry, women who refused to be spectators, who shouted from the rooftops, from courtrooms and from within the arena, how it was those with the least amount of power that saved her, who pooled their resources, with rose petals and cardamom and nard, to demonstrate to her their triumphant dissent, their refusal to participate in a power that strips them of their own power, and how a queen now gives her the most coveted wealth there is—unconditional love, and that this unconditional love she has met with outside her is ultimately a mirror for a royal power that Thecla recognizes from within her.

Whatever Thecla shares, I have to imagine it was a voice that none of them had ever heard before, a perspective about overcoming the circumstances we're born into, and a love that wakes up in others, and within us, a knowing that we are not separate from one another. Whatever Thecla says in this sermon, the scripture relates that when she finished, "Paul greatly marveled" (41:1).[3]

Then Thecla stands up and announces to Paul that she is going back to Iconium, to the small village where they first met. Paul responds by giving her the blessing now that she had asked him for long ago; Paul gives Thecla the blessing she actually no longer seeks. He says to her, "Go and teach the word of God" (41:3).[4]

What's significant about this commission from Paul is that it places Thecla in the same apostolic line as him.[5] So for example, recently, the Southern Baptist Convention expelled from their denomination all churches that were led by female minsters because, according to them, there is no scriptural precedent in the New Testament for female leadership. There is. It's right here. It's just that it wasn't included in the formation of the New Testament precisely because it is scriptural evidence of a precedent for female leadership in the church.

When Thecla reaches Iconium, instead of going to her own home, that little redbrick house depicted hundreds of years later on the walls of the Cave of Saint Paul—or the hidden virgin—she enters Onesiphorus's home. And she falls to her knees right in the place where Paul sat and told the stories about Christ that she overheard through her window next door.

In her relief, or her gratitude, or maybe just because of the magnitude of how those full-circle moments feel, Thecla starts to cry. Maybe she cries because this is the place where, before the trials, she felt she wasn't worthy enough to enter. Or maybe it's because this is the place where the words she overheard Paul sharing about Christ originated, from this house, on that floor, the words that compelled her to begin her transformation, which is now complete. For all these reasons, perhaps, Thecla starts to cry, and then she says, "God of me and of this house where the light shone on me, Christ Jesus the Child of God, my help in prison, my help before governors, my help in the fire, my help with the wild animals—you are God and you are the glory forever. Amen" (42:2).[6]

What's so enduring about Thecla's story is not only her self-mastery, and the ultimate triumph of this return home to where her story began, now as a minister herself, but also the statement her story makes within the political context of when it took place. According to scholars of the Christ Movement, the popularity and longevity of Thecla's story rests in the fact that she "resists the power of the empire, both in the presence of its officials and in its effort to destroy her in public spectacles of violence."[7] What is being celebrated here in her story is the ascendancy of the powerless.

Thecla's story takes place between two of the most critical moments in Christian history. The first moment came in the first century, when the empire crucified a Jewish peasant who inspired communities of powerless people, men and women, to see themselves as ultimately connected with and led by a power, a royal power, greater than the empire. The second moment came almost three centuries later, when Emperor Constantine recast the practices and beliefs of these communities, this Christ Movement, into the empire's religion. What makes Thecla's voice so provocative is that her individual story comes from a more ancient Christian story that pre-dates the Christianity most of us have been exposed to and taught. A Christianity that deliberately and radically shifted the meaning of who might be considered a "king," who might be deemed "savior," and who might be worthy enough to receive the spiritual authority to baptize.

The Christ Movement that Thecla's story emerges from not only existed as a safe space for those with less power but also turned the notion of "safety" on its head. In the first century, the emperor was considered the savior of Rome.[8] The savior of these communities, though, was a crucified peasant, a human man that the empire tortured and executed and attempted to humiliate and erase from history. This seemingly insignificant man within the vast power of the Roman Empire became the true savior, the true source of safety and refuge. Thecla's story then reclaims how this tradition actually began. Not as an empire's religion, but as resistance to empire. The Christ Movement hinged on the fact that the god of this crucified Judean man, the god of the defeated, of conquered nations, is in fact more powerful than any power the emperor could ever possess.

And the larger, vaster message here is that there's a wisdom, a power, that comes from the woman Christ loved the most, from the one exiled and lied about. There's a power that can only come from the girl who baptized herself. There's a voice of love we haven't yet fully heard from, a voice of the lion, the preyed upon. From the scriptures buried in the desert, torn apart, feared. The ones who have persevered because of a power that has been with them, from within them, all along. And the effort now is the opposite of the one we've focused on for millennia—it's not a rising up through the ranks, a vertical climb, a hope to reach greater amounts of power to exert over others. Here, farther up is farther in. And we rise by descending, by embodying the power of love more fully from within.

25.

The Hot Gospel

"Theocleia, Mother, can you believe that the Lord lives in heaven? For if you desire money, the Lord will give it to you through me, or your child. Look, I am standing before you."

—*The Acts of Paul and Thecla* 43:1–2

Thecla soon finds out while she's back in her hometown of Iconium that her ex-fiancé, Thamyris, is no longer living, but her mother, Theocleia, is still alive. The scripture relates that when she gets the news, Thecla "called her mother," which is the first indication that their relationship has changed. Thecla calls for her mother to come to her; she is the one who allows her mother back into her life. And when they meet, Thecla refers to her first by her name, Theocleia, before referring to her as "Mother," which speaks volumes about how much power Thecla has reclaimed.

Thecla says to her, "Theocleia, Mother, can you believe that the Lord lives in heaven? For if you desire money, the Lord will give it to you through me, or your child. Look, I am standing before you" (43:1–2).[1] Thecla here reveals the most significant power any one of us can ever possess: The power to name and define ourselves. The power that's inherent in the capacity to speak for ourselves, to use that "I am" statement that has the potential to change the trajectory of our lives depending on what comes after the declaration in those two words . . . *I am*. Thecla is no longer defined by the titles her mother's vision for her life would have demanded—dutiful daughter, obedient wife, devoted mother. Now Thecla is the author of her own story. She is the utterance of her own destiny: "I am standing before you." Thecla is now who she had always been and who her mother could never see.

Theocleia never needed to rely on a power that would oppress her with one hand and provide with the other. She never needed to sacrifice her own daughter as an example for other girls not to follow in Thecla's footsteps. She never needed to acquire her financial stability through the institution of marriage. She never needed to relinquish the potential of her own financial independence for handouts, for access to scraps of wealth and a power once removed. She never needed to be a representative, a subordinate of the patriarchy, making certain her daughter participated in the economy of worth she herself had conformed to.

Thecla is saying here to the mother who betrayed her, you could have had all that you needed through me, by believing in me, by seeing me for who I am, and by trusting that a power greater than an empire built by men exists within the heart of a little girl who is loved.

This moment when Thecla stands face-to-face with her mother is a moment that lives within us all. It's when the force that actively sought to harm us, to silence us, to kill the light inside us, is actually seen for what it truly is—a force that's outside of us and can never be as powerful as the love that saved us and brought us to this moment. The love that we carried with us all along. This is the moment when we see all the powers of the ego for what they are, ultimately illusory, ultimately powerless to the truth of love, which is what remains. After all the trials and terrors, after all the fears have passed, the emptiness, the loneliness, even if the trials return again, the love that exists within Thecla is what endures.

This moment when Thecla stands face-to-face with her mother is when we see who we've become once we've survived death, once we've walked through the flames and triumphed over the wild beasts. This is the moment when Thecla has fully embodied her power because she's now acting from it. It's when she holds all the power, not because she took that power from her mother, or from her fiancé, or from the systems of power that oppressed her. Thecla realizes through love that the power to change her life was always within her from the start. What's hers, which is endless, was always hers to claim, and can never be taken or diminished. The abundance of what Thecla has inherited hasn't come down through a lineage of external wealth; what Thecla has inherited is a wealth, a treasure that gold pales at in comparison. The inheritance Thecla has is a form of vision, of seeing what matters most in her life, and of being able to perceive where the source of true power rests.·

It would be more happy-ever-after-ish if Thecla never has to face threats and challenges again. But that's just not real. And it's not the point, that we might reach some plateau, some lofty place, and then the stuff of being human can't touch us anymore.

The whole point is to stay low to the ground, fully human, and to exist nowhere else but here. So the scripture relates that in the years to come, violent young men try to harm Thecla. They spread rumors that since she is a "maiden," she must serve Artemis, a goddess of virginity, and that "Because of this, she has power with healing" (44:1).[2]

Power is terrifying to ourselves and others. So it just makes sense that even after this moment of mastery, of facing the mother who tried to destroy her and declaring her triumphant "I am standing before you," Thecla is still at times reminded of how terrified people are of their own power, so they project their fear onto her.

I think truth is a burden until we live it. I think the weight of knowing what's actually true and real for us is a sadness, a grief that feels like a great, vast, terrifying emptiness. This is what roils beneath the Rage some express toward others who are living their truth. As if their violence says: How dare you live like this if I can't. How dare you refuse to conform. How dare you refuse to wear what your gender is meant to, or refuse to do those things acceptable for you and expected of you. How dare you be true only to yourself. How dare you demonstrate what I already know, that each and every one of us contains a power none of us can live without.

The emptiness, though, if we enter it, is just an absence. It's the terror of our own absence from this one brief life we get. It's a proximity to our own lives that scares us. Power has never been scarce. Power, the most ultimate form, belongs to all of us. And maybe this was the most dangerous suggestion these earliest believers of Christ were living out. Maybe what made Thecla such a target for men in power was that she was living proof that power doesn't only exist as a zero-sum game. Her existence crushed the old chestnut that if those with less power gain it, those with more power will lose it. Thecla's empowerment throws back the curtain and exposes this idea as just an overfed false binary. Thecla living her truth reveals what no person or institution can ever actually control—that we are each only as far from power as we are from our own embodiment.

The Gospel of Mary is ultimately about our relationship to being in a body. The limits and the possibilities. And if we're willing to stay still for long enough, face-to-face with the emptiness, we can learn to perceive what Christ refers to as the "treasure," or the "eye of the heart." This is why Mary at the beginning of her gospel says, "I will teach you about what is hidden from you" (6:3).[3] This vision, this power to know who we are, to see what's true for us in our lives, to live from a power love provides, is what has been hidden from us, and it's what we play hide-and-seek from. It's what we spend considerable amounts of energy trying not to find. Because once we know who we are, we're responsible then for living true to it.

Scripture then relates that Thecla leaves for Rome to see Paul, "and found him sleeping." And after staying by his side for a while, "she slept with a beautiful sleep. And she is buried about two or three stadia from the tomb of her teacher Paul" (44:3–4).[4]

A *stadia* is an ancient Roman measure of length of approximately 185 meters. So according to her scripture, Thecla is buried less than a mile from Paul. Then the scripture summarizes Thecla's story, her entire lifespan wrapped up in three sentences: "She was cast into the fire when she was seventeen and to the wild animals when she was eighteen. It has been said that she was an ascetic in a cave when she was seventy-two, so all the years of her life were ninety. And after accomplishing many healings, she rests in the place of the holy ones" (45:1–2).[5]

The cave is a common theme, and sometimes an actual

home, to so many mystics and saints throughout the world religions. The cave is both the literal and metaphorical space of having gone within. It's the act of shutting out the world we're born into, the world of what we can see, and literally going into the dark, like a return to the womb, to see less with the eyes the ego uses, and more with the vision darkness makes possible. To replace seeing with knowing.

There's a legend that Mary Magdalene testified to Christ's resurrection before the court of Tiberius Caesar. Supposedly Mary picked up an egg from the feast laid out before the court during her testimony. In response, Tiberius declared to her, "A body could no more resurrect than that egg in your hand turn red," and in a louder response than words could carry, the egg in Mary's hand turned red immediately. The Greek Orthodox Church still dyes eggs red on Easter—not to celebrate a fantastical egg-laying rabbit, but to remember the woman from a pre-patriarchal form of Christianity who held up an egg before the most powerful court in the empire, to testify to the invincibility of a love like Christ's.

I've always wondered why Mary used an egg as her prop to testify to the resurrection. It represents rebirth in the Passover Seder. And it's the most ancient symbol of the divine feminine. And in all the icons of Mary with an egg, she's pointing us directly to it. I've always wondered what her first sermon before the court of Tiberius Caesar might have taught us. Did she remind us that a body, like the yolk within the egg, contains a soul? Is she pointing out that it's the soul that rises? Is she reminding us that the love the soul contains, that this is what survives us? And that it's this love within us that we can rise to now—to live out our brief human lives tethered to what is eternal? That right here within us, in this human body, there is a love that never ends?

Legends relate that Mary then fled Roman persecution across the Mediterranean to a small seaside village that has been named after her, Saintes Maries-de-la-Mer. Mary is plural in the name of the village because three Marys arrived "on a ship without sails": Mary Magdalene, Mary the mother of Christ, and Mary Salome. Mary's name "the Magdalene" could refer to her title "the tower," just as Peter is "the rock." Magdalene could also refer to the fact that Mary was from the ancient town of Magdala, on the coast of the Sea of Galilee. Mary, the tower, the Magdalene, eventually went into hiding after an increase in the persecution of Christians by Roman soldiers. She fled north to Sainte Baume. And it was there that Mary spent the last thirty years of her life living in the caves along its highest peaks. This is the cave that Hesychast John Cassian consecrated after returning from Egypt in the fifth century.

The cave is symbolic for a sanctuary, a safe place, where we can shut out the external world, the chaos of trying to meet our own expectations of ourselves and the expectations of others. A place where we are forced from the weight of the silence, and the solitude, to listen foremost to what we know is true for us, to what that quiet, unassuming voice of love is constantly telling us.

The cave is something we all need, not just in our golden years like Mary and Thecla, but all throughout our lifetime. We need the cave ideally once a week, or maybe even for a small moment every day. The cave is a metaphor for the heart. And we have a great need to find our own ways of returning to it, to listen, or to light a candle there, within.

Because there's a love that's deeper than what's visible. There's a love that knows itself completely. It doesn't rely on external sight, or on anything the ego can grasp, name, or comprehend. A great unlearning has begun because of these discounted and buried scriptures that have resurfaced. And our task is clear. We need to allow that form of vision to return as a sacred part of what it has always meant to be human. So we can progress in life with discernment, to know what's compelling us, the ego or the soul.

Dr. Karen King in her translation of *The Gospel of Mary* suggests that the story of the gospel is unfinished.[6] What's so powerful about recovering these scriptures that were deemed apocryphal in the fourth century is that we have the possibility now to step into the story ourselves, to shape the totality of their combined meaning into our own time, and into our own lives.

In the wake of these recovered scriptures, we can extend Christianity's roots back further than when it formed at the request of an emperor. It can return to the soil of how it all began in a movement that challenged, not reinforced, external forms of power. Back to the original movement that suggested no matter how things look from the outside, no matter how complete the devastation, there is a power that exists within us, latent though it may seem, that is a form of vision, a direct knowing, and that it's this vision that has ultimate sovereignty. Because it's the vision love offers us in every lifetime, and in each next generation, to make new choices, to dare to move the story of what it might mean to be human forward.

The Acts of Paul and Thecla ends with this final sentence, a praise and a promise: "In Christ Jesus, our Lord, to whom be the glory and strength forever and ever. Amen" (45:2).[7]

On New Year's Day, Jacob from the bible came to visit me in the home I had moved to after the miracle of that holy shift from Cleveland—to a small barrier island in the South, in a region called the Treasure Coast. He had just finished his new album, so we drove to the ocean to listen to it all the way through, with the volume cranked up as high as my car's sound system could go, while watching the wind make jagged white cliffs of the waves.

A song came on, and from the moment it first started, it catalyzed a never-felt-before emotion in me. I felt in equal measure this heavy depth, this gravity from the harm religion has caused so many for so long, and also, simultaneously, a winged sensation, the highest possible elation, from the love that liberates. And I knew, by the end of the song, that it was Thecla's anthem. It's called "The Hot Gospel."

A couple of days later, I woke up in the middle of the night with this dramatic gasp. I had this sense suddenly of having realized something profound, but all that I realized was that it was the third of January. The number three, though, felt lit up, bedazzled, as if it were glowing, neon and proud. It made me think of Thecla, of transformation and rebirth, and then it finally hit me—I realized I had been sober-sober for three years. Three years of choosing not to "exist elsewhere." Three years of not turning back, of being my own. And somehow between then and when I woke up the next morning, I just knew that today, the third, was the day I was meant to baptize myself.

Once I figured it out, it felt as though it had been intended all along. It was why Jacob from the bible felt so compelled to come visit me. It was why I had asked my mom to save my grandmother's wedding dress for me years ago. It's why it was hanging in my closet right now. To wear it that morning. Into the ocean. So while Jacob was sipping his tea and writing on the patio, I slipped into her white lace gown and came out of my bedroom ready to go. His face lit up with recognition as soon as he saw me—he instantly understood the assignment.

The hardest part was not looking back as I walked into the waves. The urge was so visceral, so deeply embedded into what's human in me. Facing a rebirth like this, a baptism. I wanted the comfort, the reassurance, of seeing what still remained. Jacob from the bible somehow anticipated this, so he read a passage from a book I love, titled *Talking with Angels,* before I hugged him and started walking toward the water:

> You have come to the end of the way;
> there is no more way.
> You look for a place to put down your foot
> and you see nothing.
> Nothing is there . . . because you look.
> The eye no longer exists for looking, as before.
> Look no more with the old eye.
> And there will be a new way under your feet.[8]

The ocean was wild and passionate that morning. It was a sea meant only for the unambiguous. I knew there was a reason it called to me and not a lake or a river. I commit with tenacity. Resolve. Baptism by high seas just made sense to me; it matches my intensity. So I didn't look back as fiercely as I wanted to. I walked slowly, deliberately, one foot after the next, into the waves in my grandmother's wedding dress while Jacob from the bible sang "The Hot Gospel" from the shore.

What's next for me is what I haven't known before. This is my line in the sand. This is my public display of reclaiming a power that has always existed within me. What's next for me is a devotion to what exists within me in a way I've never known before. It's a wedded self I claim, a wholeness of both the little girl who protected herself by leaving her body, and the woman who's walking into the ocean now fully committed to existing nowhere else but right here, within.

As the waves began to reach my feet, I remembered a quote

that felt like my first clue, my first breadcrumb that had led me to this moment. Before I found *The Gospel of Mary* or *The Acts of Paul and Thecla,* these words from the third-century Egyptian philosopher Plotinus read like a signpost: "Shut your eyes and evoke another way of seeing which everyone has but few use."[9]

The wind carried the chorus of Jacob's lyrics to me even when I was far enough out to be waist deep in seawater: "Do the hot gospel, do the bad believer, do the broken healer, do the saint, do the spell, do the heaven, do the hell, do the hot gospel." His presence made me think of the "*with*-ness" of the groups that comprised the Christ Movement, the with-ness that made my life so infinitely filled with connection. And that it's this practice of "being with" each other, with a love that's greater than all of us, and also within each one of us—this is how everything changes. This is how I understand what bell hooks might mean when she writes, "Healing is an act of communion."[10]

Being with those who recognize this love that resides within us. Being with those who help us remember when we forget, which is what it means to be human—that we have always been and will always remain worthy of embodying it.

There's a law in physics called the conservation of energy, which essentially means that energy cannot be created or destroyed, only converted. This is the kind of conversion experience I had as I neared the depth I wanted to reach, and a wave came careening past me. All that love that had felt unmet and unrequited for so many years transformed. It was realized as a love that loves through me, and whether it's ever met or reciprocated isn't ultimately the point. The point is that this love resides within me. The point is remaining who I am, not becoming someone else by severing myself from it. After all these years, it's the triumph of still being able to choose it. It's the triumph of not letting the world alter the person I am from within. It's standing before everything hard and horrific that has happened in my life in a white lace gown as if repeating with conviction this truth that Thomas Merton found: "Love is the non-stop body of believing."[11]

This is the life of my own choosing. This is how I resist a world that wants me distracted, focused outward. This is how I keep from being misled by what happens, again and again, in the world around me. This is how I remain still from here on out, and move from that power that exists within. That power of love that has been *with* me all along.

This is how I find what can't be told.

This is how I find what already exists within me. It's a diamond, a well. It's an unspeakable light, a vat of honey. It has no better name except home. And it calls to me when I'm lonely, when I feel not enough, that I haven't yet given back to the world the joy I feel just to exist in it. When I'm confused, tangled again, not seeing clearly, mired in the ego's power. When I can't see the feast of choices laid out before me, or the power I have to create a new one.

It's here waiting. This knowing. This world within this one. A world that's merciful. This way of being here that's the most radical, because its source doesn't depend on anything external to me.

It's what glimmers in my eyes when the word "defeated" overwhelms me, when I'm filled to the gills with the word "failure." It's there when I'm drowning in regret, or shame is coursing through me—I catch this light in my eyes, and I know again in that place where words no longer have meaning, I know that everything is going to be all right. Not because it is. But because there's nothing that exists outside of me that this love within me cannot meet.

Just as the lyric to the last chorus reached me, "Do the hot gospel, cuz I got god in my heart still," I said confidently, with my eyes closed, "In the name of Jesus Christ, I baptize myself."

And when I went under, I didn't come back up the same.

CONCLUSION

A Very Few People

Love has never been a popular movement, and no one's ever
wanted really to be free. The world is held together, really it is,
held together, by the love and the passion of a very few people.

—James Baldwin

Within these communities that formed in secret among the most oppressed in Roman society in the Christ Movement, scholars believe that the earliest forms of Christian worship were the supper clubs they created. And the most common ritual for their worship was the humble yet significant language of food, breaking bread together, providing sustenance for one another.

It was during these ritual gatherings to share a meal that these Christ communities would announce their own form of "good news," taking their defiant turn to the empire's practice of proclaiming the good news of battles won, of more land taken, more countries overthrown, and more people enslaved. Instead of what's good according to the rulers, the supper club members of the Christ Movement redefined what was actually good according to the ruled. The everyday victories, the shred of light amidst unimaginable suffering, the quiet, unassuming moments of triumph in their lives that existed for them like a rivulet of gold in cement. This is what they fed each other—infinite moments of joy amidst vast and pervasive suffering.

My first spiritual community began decades ago with a small group of women, sitting on the floor of my apartment, eating takeout after work and saying all the things we had never been able to say out loud before about god, about religion, about what we really wanted in marriage, about sex and children, about how much more magic and possibility we knew existed for us. All the taboo things were permissible and invited. We called ourselves the REDLADIES, and instead of bread, we broke dark chocolate. This small group of women changed me, because they met me where I was. And I was done with participating in any form of deception that to be human was anything less than miraculous. I was done with any form of spiritual authority extolling patriarchy as scripture. I was done with being controlled by this concept of what might be considered holy as decreed by men two millennia ago. I had met the women who had also called bullshit on the misogyny they found in their lives and places of worship. I had met my band of outsiders. My supper club. Long before I found out about the ancient history of them years later in seminary.

When I moved to New York City for graduate school, another small group of REDLADIES started to gather. And through the years, what became clear to me is how I understand what James Baldwin might have meant when he said that "love has never been a popular movement."[1] The reality of love insists on equity for all of us. The reality of love demands that we show up for one another, and that we listen. It means telling the truth according to our own experience, not some story we've been forced to memorize and recite since age three. It means doing the hard work of digging through the lies we've settled with about ourselves and getting to the truth beneath them. The truth about what really matters, about what's still possible for us, about what we really want as women, as human beings, about how motherhood is everything to some of us, and how it's an oppressive and antiquated expectation to others.

What became clear to me in these circles of women about what James Baldwin may have meant by "no one's ever really wanted to be free" is that the possibility to get free has always been right here. Within and in-between us. From time spent being with each other, committed to each other. Within a small group of a very few people, we can receive the love that liberates us from the ideas, concepts, and illusions that have kept us from seeing who we really are. Already. As is. Not in some distant future once we've "become more." Now. As broken bits of the universe already prepackaged with an infinite spark. Most of us say we want to be free, as in mentally and emotionally free, as in free from the egoic states or powers that bind us daily. We say this, but then we snuggle up with an Excess that has comforted us for years. And we prefer that sleep, rather than the dull, disturbing ache of what it might feel like to wake up without it.

REDLADIES eventually grew too large for my living room floor and morphed into a conference called REVEAL. It was a conference for women of all different religious and spiritual backgrounds to come together and talk about what's sacred and holy for them; what god is in their experience. To confer and question the spiritual practices that really liberate us. We met annually for several years, first in the chapel of Union

Theological Seminary, then at Donna Karan's Urban Zen, and finally at NYU's Global Center for Academic and Spiritual Life. Luminaries like Sikh storyteller and activist Valerie Kaur, Black maternal health advocate and doula Latham Thomas, and spiritual teacher Gabby Bernstein graced REVEAL's stage. Lifelong bonds were formed from telling the truth about our lives. And by sharing the truth, shame just visibly lifted from us. And we danced, which is what I remember most vividly. I've titled those memories from all three years "How Women Pray When No One Else Is Watching."

REVEAL morphed into my first book, then eventually an international spiritual community that's currently called The House of Mary Magdalene. We study together the scripture originally left out of the New Testament, the ones mentioned in this book, like *The Gospel of Mary, The Acts of Paul and Thecla, The Gospel of Thomas,* and *The Thunder: Perfect Mind.* We refer to scholar and pastor Hal Taussig's *A New New Testament* as our sacred text. And we practice meditating together, to try, as Christ instructs Mary in her gospel, to see with the *nous,* the spiritual eye of the heart.

I was recently back in Cleveland supporting my dad, who is technically my stepdad, but that title has never described him. Mostly, I refer to him as my best friend ever; this is how his number is saved in my cellphone. My BFE was having surgery to remove his kidney, which had in a very stealthy way become consumed with cancer.

I was meditating like the Hesychasts, camped out in my heart, and being prayed in that lady boss imperative mood. I was doing all the things. And still. I think I also only now understand what James Baldwin might have meant when he said, "The world is held together, really it is, held together, by the love and the passion of a very few people." Because I sent a group text to MANNA the night before my BFE's surgery, and got really human with how much I needed prayers for him, and also for me. And the love I received in return, the prayers they prayed, the love they sent, it was so much that it didn't sink in until I was headed back home to the Treasure Coast. I was stopped at a red light when suddenly a huge food truck came up right beside me. MANNA was written in gigantic letters across the whole side of it.

MANNA. My face finally flooded with all the emotion that's too much of an unsayable mix of love overwhelming grief. This is how we keep going, how we keep from burning out or giving up. This is how we keep believing in a world that's here, that's possible. When we're spent, and out past any known pain we've encountered before, it's the love and passion of a very few people that keeps us tethered right here to it. This is how I am fed. In these moments of pure joy amidst deep suffering like rivulets of gold in cement.

I found a quote recently in a book by psychiatrist Marion Woodman, titled *The Pregnant Virgin*. I've read it cover to cover over the years too many times to count—my red ink circling and highlighting the most critical parts. And yet somehow I never saw this quote until now: "The abandoned one at the heart of the addiction is the soul of the potentially conscious woman, the virgin, 'one-in-herself.' She is the one who needs food. Her food is the food of the creative imagination."[2]

My local supper club is comprised of three women, who all live on this little island with me. One of them—named Grace, of course—attended a REVEAL from a decade ago; she reached out to me as soon as I arrived. And from our first meeting, it was as if all the work I've ever done, all the healing, and also all the scholarship, all the traveling alone as a pilgrim for all those years, all the circles of women I facilitated, all the love I had ever extended to restore the divine feminine, came back to me in the form of these three women. Jacob from the bible told us about how, in 1896, the Swedish artist and mystic Hilma af Klint began to meet with four of her female friends who weren't feeling spiritually content, or satisfied, with traditional church services. They prayed together, meditated, and interpreted a sermon from the New Testament. They called themselves "The Five." So our group text thread is named "The Four."

Existing nowhere else but here, within, takes creativity, imagination. It takes being able to discern what truly nourishes you. What gives you the strength and the courage to continue to be there for yourself, to be the one who refuses to abandon you. What practices, what rituals, what litany of "Blessed ares." What helps you trust what your body is telling you. And what gives you the perception to recognize your chosen family, who can remind you of the answers you already contain. Who are the people that are meant to practice with you that most ancient form of worship—feeding one another and ourselves that "invisible light of heaven."

This is what I want most for you. I want the love of a very few people to surround you. I want you to be fed by the singular freedom their love can offer you. I want you to focus not on finding the one but the many, the people who will want more for you than you even know how to want for yourself. I want you to have a small group that you can announce your good news to, people who want to celebrate with you those moments in life that we might otherwise overlook, or fail to notice, so that the sacred doesn't pass us by undetected. I want you to have a community that helps you see what's still possible for you, and helps you know the love within you that will save you. I want you to have the love of a very few people, because it is in the practice of being with their love that your own world is transfixed and transformed.

ACKNOWLEDGMENTS

The root system beneath this book is vast, from the teachings of the saints, mystics, and troublemakers within the world religions who never failed to call god love, even when it got them burned at the stake for it, to the feminist and liberation theologians who have written about a love that liberates even if it meant being imprisoned or exiled from the church for it; I am a writer because of the words that have survived you. Mary Magdalene, Thecla, Perpetua, Marguerite Porete, Joan of Arc, William Blake, William James, Rainer Maria Rilke, Simone Weil, Dr. Martin Luther King, Jr., Thomas Merton, James Baldwin, Gitta Mallasz, Audre Lorde, Dr. Marija Gimbutas, Dr. Marie-Louise von Franz, Mary Daly, Dr. Jane Schaberg, Marion Woodman, and bell hooks.

Dr. Judith Plascow, Starhawk, Dr. Carol Lee Flinders, Sue Monk Kidd, Dr. Elaine Pagels, China Galland, Dr. Diana Eck, Dr. Cornel West, Dr. Jeffrey J. Kripal, Dr. Karen L. King, Dr. Elisabeth Schüssler Fiorenza, Sister Joan Chittister, Dr. Leila Ahmed, Dr. Hal Taussig, Dr. Hyung Chung, Dr. Robert Thurman, Dr. James Cone, Jean-Yves Leloup, Dr. Robert Holden, and Dr. Cynthia Bourgeault for the red thread your work offered me through the labyrinth.

Jamia Wilson for the absolute magic of being in REDLADIES

with you all those years ago, for being a witness with me to the power of REVEAL, and for knowing that everything has been leading to this collaboration to make Thecla famous.

Ethan for the expertise in church history you wove into the copyedits, and Miriam for your tech-savvy support with unruly endnotes, and to the entire Random House team, it feels meant to be for *The Girl* to be published with you.

Rebecca Gradinger for pushing me to write with searing clarity from the start, and for advocating for Thecla, for knowing the worth of bringing her story back from erasure.

Rahiel Tesfamariam for showing up week after week to write our book proposals together as sister theologians, and for "this is love work we are doing here—for generations of women to come." Van Jones for believing in me, and for "this is just the beginning." Lilakoi Moon for the way you infuse your soul in all you do, and for the way you gently, fiercely, set mine on fire. And for "with, not for or against, or on or off, on top, under, before, or after, with all that is."

Iyanla Vanzant for telling me at the most divinely timed moment to "keep writing."

The Omega Institute for inviting me, along with Jake Wesley Rogers and Traci Jackson, to co-lead the Mary Magdalene Revealed Retreat. Jake for "there is only one thing 'artist' means: harbinger," and "give 'em heaven." Traci for teaching me the "fists of rage" kriya that renovated my entire nervous system.

Glennon Doyle and Abby Wambach for inviting me to speak for the first time about Thecla during your retreat at the Omega Institute the summer before the world stood still.

The House of Mary Magdalene for being the community I've always needed.

Gabby Bernstein for the FaceTime that kept me from turning back ever again.

Paul William Morris for believing in me as a writer before I did.

Elise Loehnen for our itty-bitty book club.

Tele Darden for helping me reach across a great distance to heal what I couldn't alone.

Angela King, Grace Smith, and Katy Corrigan for being my long-lost ladyloves, and for being my version of Hilma af Klint's "The Four."

Kate Northrup because we get to have this ladylove, and Kate Fisher just because.

Tom Gattusso for finding me the home I recognized immediately, and for being an irreplaceable family friend and source of support.

Guillaume Daporta for being a presence of love even in the absence of it.

Liz Wheeler Kosh for being the most loving little sister and for giving me the most adorable tiny feminist niece in Em Margaret Kosh.

Margaret Wheeler for teaching me to seek the good in everyone and in all things, and for knowing and supporting the feminist I was always meant to become.

David Watterson for doing the hard, healing work sobriety demands, and for being a critical support as I did my own work to get sober-sober.

Shai Watterson Masi for being the greatest gift my life has ever known, and the greatest teacher of a love that's too infinite for me to find adequate words to ever name.

Joseph Masi for trying so many times and for so many years to love me with a love that stays, and for being the one to lead me finally to the love within that endures, and remains.

Best Friend Ever for demonstrating to all of us what integrity looks like, and for believing in the worth of the words I've spent my life devoted to bringing forth from within me.

The Girl Who Baptized Herself

PREFACE: BAPTIZE

"Love has never been a popular movement."

—James Baldwin

Why was it so dangerous to be Christian before the fourth century?

Do I identify as a feminist?

What is Watterson's definition of feminism?

What is feminist theology?

What rituals hold meaning for me in my life?

What does it mean for me to be baptized?

What does it mean to be baptized within the context of Thecla's story?

Introduction

1. HER NAME

"The only way out is within."

—Watterson

Are there aspects of Christian history that I struggle to reconcile?

What does the phrase "the love that liberates" mean to me?

What is my experience and understanding of Christ's teachings?

What is the Christ Movement?

What does the existence of *The Acts of Paul and Thecla* suggest about the Christ Movement?

How have I been seeing out through a small window in my life?

What is an example of a cage my ego has held me comfortably captive within?

What is Watterson's intention in sharing Thecla's story?

---

2. WITHIN

"The definition of insanity is doing the same thing over and over and expecting different results."

—Narcotics Anonymous

Is there a choice I keep making because I think it will turn out differently, but it never does?

What does Rilke mean by advising "go into yourself and . . . examine the depths from which your life springs"?

What makes the spiritual transformation in Thecla's story different from the hero's journey?

What are the seven stages of spiritual transformation in *The Acts of Paul and Thecla*?

What is the ultimate goal of the spiritual transformation in Thecla's story?

The First Stage

---

3. ERASURE

"With Thecla restored from erasure, with the hidden virgin now visible again, we know that the nature of the call demands that it exclude no one. Because this call is a call to love, and it comes from within."

—Watterson

Why is this scene of Thecla sitting by her window depicted in the Cave of Saint Paul so significant to her story?

What did I know about Paul before reading this chapter?

What did I know about Thecla before reading this chapter?

Why does Watterson believe there are conflicting messages in the scripture attributed to Paul?

What is an example of a recent wake-up call in my life?

What crisis or loss in my life can I reframe now as an initiation to go inward?

4. A LOVE THAT LIBERATES

"The word 'kingdom' is translated into English from the Greek word *vasileio* or *basileio*, which can also be translated as 'royal power.'"

—Watterson

How would I describe what it's like to be fully loved?

What does Watterson mean by "the heart's heart"?

Why did Watterson serve as a chaplain in the neonatal intensive care unit (NICU)?

What is another way to translate "the kingdom of god"?

Have I experienced "the love that liberates"?

What makes love liberational?

5. THE WORD

"Power can be defined as the ability to make a particular perspective seem universal."

—Alok Vaid-Menon

What does the expression "the word of god" mean to me?

Do I believe in the theological concept of original sin?

Who was Saint Augustine?

Does a saint's misogyny factor into his theology?

Who is considered "the Father of Latin Theology"?

Why is the Council of Nicaea in 325 C.E. significant?

Why is the Council of New Orleans in 2012 also significant, and how did it differ from the Council of Nicaea?

---

6. YES & NO & MAYBE

"I am the whore and the holy woman. I am the wife and the virgin. I am the bride and the bridegroom. I am she, the lord."

—*The Thunder: Perfect Mind*

What does the word "exegesis" mean?

Do I think scripture is meant to be read literally?

What is my process for interpreting scripture?

What is *The Thunder: Perfect Mind,* and why was it included in *A New New Testament*?

What is the Greek word *nous* and how does it relate to *The Thunder: Perfect Mind*?

What does Watterson mean by "yes and no and maybe"?

How did the Christ Movement challenge gender norms within the Roman Empire?

---

7. VOICE

"What you say, you say in a body. You can say nothing outside this body. You must awaken while in this body, for everything exists in it: Resurrect in this life."

—*The Gospel of Philip*

What voice has been the predominant voice for interpreting scripture for the past two millennia, and why is this so significant?

Has the experience of my embodiment informed my ideas of god?

If I listen within, what is "that one little piece that wants to be spoken out"?

What are the spiritual practices that allow me to hear the voice of my soul?

8. POWER

"To be a Christian is to live dangerously, honestly, freely—to step in the name of love as if you may land on nothing, yet to keep on stepping because the something that sustains you no empire can give you and no empire can take away."

—Dr. Cornel West

What does the expression "fruits of justice" signify?

Are there people in my life I recognized—as if they seemed familiar even when I first met them?

Is there a time when I felt as if I experienced what I thought church might be, but in an unexpected place?

Have I ever prayed for something and felt that same warning surface as it did for Watterson, "Be careful what you wish for"?

Do I think spirituality and activism can be or ever have been separate?

Can I think of examples when I gave my power away to a person or an institution?

9. PURITY

"Blessed are you that you did not waver at seeing me. For where the mind is, there is the treasure."

—*The Gospel of Mary*

What does the word "purity" mean to me?

How do I interpret the passage "Blessed are the clear of heart, for they will see god"?

What does the Greek word *anthropos* mean? How is it relevant when encountering concepts like purity and virginity?

What is the ancient practice of remembrance, or *anamnesis*?

What is *kenosis*?

Is there a time when I didn't have a choice about what happened to my body?

If I could write my own "Blessed ares," what would they be?

The Second Stage

10. WORTH

"As yet we see, in a mirror, dimly, but then—face-to-face! As yet my knowledge is incomplete, but then I will know in full, as I have been fully known."

—1 Corinthians 13:12

Why is it significant to understand how Thecla is described and defined by the word "maiden"?

What does Watterson mean by "an economy of worth"?

Why does reclaiming our worth play such a crucial role in the process of transformation?

If there is a reliquary behind my heart, what relics or memories does it hold for me?

Why is "doing nothing" so significant in this stage of transformation?

11. THE BODY'S BODY

"It's the choice that's sacred."

—Watterson

Have I had less access to choices in my life because of who I am?

Have I ever felt what it was like to be treated as a commodity?

What is the spiritual significance of the number three?

Who am I if I am not pleasing anyone?

Who am I if I am just alive for myself—if I have no titles or names that signify my worth?

The Third Stage

12. COURAGE

"Until the lions have their own historians, the history of the hunt will always glorify the hunter."

—Chinua Achebe

Am I the subject of my own story?

Do I see myself as breaking new ground in some aspect of my life, and if so, how? If not, what would I like to see happen in my life or in the world that hasn't yet?

Is there a "new desire" I feel in this moment for my life?

What does Watterson mean by suggesting "we haven't heard yet fully what god is for the lion, only the hunter"?

What does the lionized heart sound like for me?

13. PURPOSE

"I am here for my purpose. I'm not here to make people comfortable or to be liked. My purpose is to know and experience love. This means excavating the unsaid. In the world and in me."

—Brené Brown

How does the Greek word *anthropos* relate to our purpose?

What is our true purpose in being human according to *The Gospel of Mary*?

Have I ever heard the voice that Watterson describes as "standing up" like Mary and comforting doubt and disbelief—a voice of love in the midst of terror?

What have I been called crazy for believing in or for trying to make happen that others don't think is possible?

What do I know is my purpose?

The Fourth Stage

14. POSSESSION

"Love is the opposite of control."

—Watterson

What is the traditional modern-day list of the seven deadly sins?

What's the most fundamental difference between the seven powers in Mary's gospel and the seven deadly sins?

What are the three stages of the mystical path according to the Christian monk John Cassian?

What is the definition of "possession"?

How does possession relate to the seven powers?

15. LOVE

"The desire to be loved is the last illusion: give it up and you will be free."

—Margaret Atwood

How is Watterson distinguishing between two different expressions of love in this chapter?

Do I *know* love, as in, have I experienced it directly from within me?

When did the concept of marriage begin, and what was its original function?

When did marriage become a sacrament?

What is the truest truth I can say about what I desire when it comes to love?

Do I feel conscious or aware of a worthiness to be loved whether I am with a partner or not?

Can I choose to be on my own if I want or need to be?

16. NAKEDNESS

"You mistook the garment I wore for my true self. And you did not recognize me."

—The Gospel of Mary

Why is it so significant that Thecla refuses to answer her mother and fiancé?

What does the spiritual motif of nakedness signify?

Why is it so important that Thecla takes off her bracelets and gives away her silver mirror?

What is an example of practicing *kenosis*?

Why does Thecla again refuse to answer the governor when he orders her to answer him?

How is Thecla's silence a rebellion?

What does Thecla's mother fully embody in this chapter?

Are there ways that I "exist elsewhere" in order to numb or dull a painful situation or experience in my life?

The Fifth Stage

---

17. DEATH

"You cannot see my face, for no one may see my face and live."

—Exodus

What is Watterson's definition of vulnerability?

How is vulnerability a powerful strength?

What does it mean to be a witness?

How do we build a church that extends back to the Christ Movement that existed before it?

Is there a pattern I am ready to die to in my life? Or is there a cage I can clearly see now that my ego created, and that I am ready to free myself from?

What is Watterson's feminist list of the seven powers from *The Gospel of Mary*?

What is the rage that clarifies? And why is this form of rage so sacred?

How do we dismantle the systemic abuses of power within the church?

Have I felt mercy for myself the way Watterson describes in this chapter?

---

18. PRAYER

"I think there is something cosmic or superhuman smoldering in the human, something that seems ready to burst into flames, and sometimes does."

—Jeffrey J. Kripal

What does Watterson mean by using a "lady boss tone" in prayer?

What is the connection to prayer and the clarity of the heart?

What was the aim of the Hesychasts?

What did Hesychasts repeat within the heart?

Have I ever experienced Watterson's description of "being prayed"?

Why does Paul refuse to baptize Thecla when she asks him to?

Do I have a form of meditation practice, even if unconventional?

How do I define a miracle?

Have I experienced miracles in my life?

The Sixth Stage

19. SACRED RAGE

"Good does not mean obedient."

—Watterson

What is so powerful within the context of the first century about Thecla's declaration to Alexander of Syria as he attacks her, "I am important among the Iconians"?

Why was it so unimaginable for a woman in the first century to fight back to protect herself?

How do I make sense of this cryptic passage from *The Thunder: Perfect Mind*?: "What is your inside is your outside . . . and what you see on the outside, you see revealed on the inside."

In what ways does Thecla begin to demonstrate protecting the treasure she has realized is within her?

How is goodness inherent rather than performative, according to *The Gospel of Mary*?

What enrages me most right now in my life, and in the world?

What does this rage inform me about the pith of what most concerns me?

20. SACRILEGE

"This is the true sacrilege, in the first century as much as it is in the twenty-first—suggesting that Thecla doesn't own or know her own body and doesn't get to live the life she wills for herself."

—Watterson

Why is it important to really question and become clear about what I hold most sacred?

What does "surrender" mean to Watterson as a survivor of assault?

What is the consciousness Watterson met with in the midst of terror?

Have I ever encountered the power that Watterson articulates rising from within when I felt externally at my least powerful?

What does the lion symbolize in Thecla's story?

Why is it so significant that it's the women and the children who cry out for Thecla's freedom?

21. AUTHORITY

"Freeing yourself was one thing, claiming ownership of that freed self was another."

—Toni Morrison

How do I begin to trust the voice I can only hear from within?

Have I claimed ownership of my freed self as Toni Morrison illuminates?

What does spiritual authority mean to me? What does it look and feel like in my life?

Why is it so critical in Thecla's story that she baptizes herself?

How does Thecla's baptism directly challenge the patriarchy?

How does this patriarchal paradigm of power that the church was built on create a breeding ground for abuses of power within it?

How would I describe the god of my own understanding?

22. FREEDOM

"What is freedom but the ability to answer this question: 'Who are you?' And what is freedom but the capacity to then live out the answer?"

—Watterson

How do the women in the crowd respond when Thecla baptizes herself?

How would I personally answer the question the governor asks Thecla in the arena: Who are you?

Who were the Enslaved of God?

How did the early Christ Movement as a community directly challenge the empire's structure of power?

The Seventh Stage

23. THE WOMEN ALL CRIED OUT IN A LOUD VOICE

"There's a timeless formula found here in this scripture: No amount of powerlessness is without power once unified."

—Watterson

Why is it significant that Thecla explains she is not being "clothed" by the empire as she takes the clothes the governor offers?

What does it mean to "clothe ourselves with the perfect Human," according to *The Gospel of Mary*?

What did "good news" mean to the people of the early Christ Movement?

Why is it so significant that the scripture relates that it's the women in the crowd who "all cried out in a loud voice, as if from one mouth"?

What does the queen symbolize or represent in the process of Thecla's transformation?

Why is that moment when Thecla and the queen embrace so symbolically significant?

Have I experienced both the patriarchal mother and the mother freed from the patriarchy?

Can I imagine becoming or embodying the queen, and mothering myself with unconditional love?

24. THE GIRL WHO BAPTIZED HERSELF

"There's a power that can only come from the girl who baptized herself."

—Watterson

What are the implications of the fact that Thecla created her own garment, "a robe in the fashion of a man's"?

Why is Thecla's comment to Paul after she baptizes herself so significant?

If I had to imagine Thecla's first sermon, when Paul asks her to preach not only to the people following her, but also to everyone following him, what do I think she might have said?

What is so critical about Paul's statement to Thecla after she preaches her first sermon, "Go and teach the word of God"?

Why do I think Thecla cries when she reaches the place where she first heard Paul teach about Christ?

Why do scholars believe Thecla's story was so popular?

Is Thecla's story personally relevant to me?

Why is Thecla's voice so significant in the history of Christianity?

25. THE HOT GOSPEL

"Healing is an act of communion."

—bell hooks

Why is the return home so crucial in Thecla's story?

Have I had a moment like Thecla's where I've come face-to-face with someone who harmed me, and I was able to say my own version of "I am standing before you"?

What does the cave symbolize in both Mary Magdalene's and Thecla's story?

Can I imagine carving out time to go into the "cave" as Watterson describes?

What does Watterson mean by a practice of "being with"?

How is healing "an act of communion," as bell hooks suggests?

Conclusion: A Very Few People

"The world is held together, really it is, held together, by the love and passion of a very few people."

—James Baldwin

What was the earliest known form of worship in the Christ Movement?

What was so subversive about the supper clubs of the Christ Movement?

Can I imagine creating a community of "a very few people" to share "good news" with and to dine together, whether the nourishment is literal or figurative or both?

Do I already have a community of "a very few people" that I can see now and recognize as a beloved community?

Can I find ways to come together with them and support them as they listen and follow the "new desire" their soul is calling them to act on?

What art, activism, or offering can I imagine bringing forth from within me with the support of this supper club?

SOUL-VOICE MEDITATION
(THREE INTENTIONAL BREATHS)

The soul-voice meditation is deceptively simple. It's a way to know what's true for you. It's a way to practice *kenosis,* emptying the egoic self, for the soul to come through. And all it takes is three intentional breaths.

An intentional breath is just setting an intention to a breath you take. See, simple. And you keep breathing normally in between the three intentional breaths.

The first intentional breath is to go inward—which is an act of sealing out the external world and powering down the incessant chatter in the mind. It's an act of descending beneath the surface noise of the egoic thoughts and the constant distraction they offer us. It's an act of sinking deep below to where there is always calm (even when we're the most riled up). It's reaching down to where there's stillness at the center of what we comprehend as our core, the truth of who we are, even as everything whirls around us in perpetual change.

The second intentional breath is for once we're there, within. And this breath calls us to the presence of the soul. If "soul" is a word too bizarre-sounding to you, or if it feels too distant to be a part of you, much less existing in some nondescript place in your body's body, then the true self might name it for you. Or just the presence of love. All that matters is that you meet with it. Or more than that—all that matters is that with the second breath, there's a sense of merging with it. Of somehow recognizing it and sensing that you are not separate from it. That you know this love is the actual essence of who you are.

Then, from that place of union, ask any question that comes to you. And wait for the answer. Listening typically has three challenges. First, we *think* we already know the answer. So each time we hear something, we discard or discount it because we're waiting for the answer we came into the meditation already clutching on to. Second, we don't believe we could be this powerful. That we could have the power to ask a question within us and receive the answer. So, even when we hear something powerful, something significant, we never act on it. The third challenge is that we aren't fully aware yet of the way that listening is also a form of seeing.

If I ask, for example, what do I need to know in this moment (a classic icebreaker for you and your soul), the answer may arrive in a voice that comes from within, in a series of images—like watching a film suddenly with the back of the eyelids as the projector screen, or in a wash of emotion that tells its own wordless story, and that generates a healing just from the finality or completion of allowing yourself to be present for it, to feel it fully. Seeing with the eye of the heart is about perception; it's about a form of perceiving the answers that come parading through us when we can get still enough, and clear enough, to receive them.

The third intentional breath is to return, hopefully more present now, and more connected to that love that waits within to guide us. And the red thread you can tie around your wrist is a reminder, a visual of the unseen truth that you are tethered to this love, to the soul of who you are. That you are trying, never perfectly but authentically, to bring forth what is within you, because you've remembered, as Christ states in *The Gospel of Thomas,* that "what is within you will save you."

For more, visit www.megganwatterson.com
to download a guided soul-voice meditation.

READING LIST
(WORDS THAT FEED THE INVISIBLE LIGHT INSIDE YOU)

Baldwin, James. *The Fire Next Time*. New York: Vintage Books, 1962.

Bourgeault, Cynthia. *Eye of the Heart: A Spiritual Journey into the Imaginal Realm*. Boulder, Colo.: Shambhala Publications, 2020.

———. *The Meaning of Mary Magdalene: Discovering the Woman at the Heart of Christianity*. Boulder, Colo.: Shambhala Publications, 2010.

Chittister, Sister Joan. *Heart of Flesh: Feminist Spirituality for Women and Men*. Grand Rapids, Mich.: Eerdmans, 1998.

Doyle, Glennon. *Untamed*. New York: Dial Press, 2020.

Ehrman, Bart. *Lost Scriptures: Books That Did Not Make It into the New Testament*. New York: Oxford University Press, 2003.

Flinders, Carol Lee. *At the Root of This Longing: Reconciling a Spiritual Hunger and a Feminist Thirst*. New York: HarperOne, 1999.

hooks, bell. *Communion: The Female Search for Love*. New York: William Morrow, 2002.

———. *All About Love: New Visions*. New York: William Morrow, 2018.

Johnson, Scott Fitzgerald. *The Life and Miracles of Thekla: A Literary Study*. Boston: Center for Hellenic Studies, Harvard University Press, 2006.

Jones, Van. *The Green Collar Economy: How One Solution Can Fix Our Two Biggest Problems*. New York: HarperOne, 2008.

King, Karen. *The Gospel of Mary of Magdala: Jesus and the First Woman Apostle*. Santa Rosa, Calif.: Polebridge Press, 2003.

Klein, Linda Kay. *Pure: Inside the Evangelical Movement That Shamed a Generation of Young Women and How I Broke Free*. New York: Atria Books, 2019.

Kripal, Jeffrey J. *Roads of Excess, Palaces of Wisdom: Eroticism & Reflexivity in the Study of Mysticism.* Chicago: University of Chicago Press, 2001.

―――. *The Serpent's Gift: Gnostic Reflections on the Study of Religion.* Chicago: University of Chicago Press, 2007.

―――. *The Superhumanities: Historical Precedents, Moral Objections, New Realities.* Chicago: University of Chicago Press, 2022.

Leloup, Jean-Yves. *The Gospel of Mary Magdalene.* Rochester, Vt.: Inner Traditions, 2002.

―――. *The Gospel of Philip: Jesus, Mary Magdalene, and the Gnosis of Sacred Union.* Rochester, Vt.: Inner Traditions, 2003.

Loehnen, Elise. *On Our Best Behavior: The Seven Deadly Sins and the Price Women Pay to Be Good.* New York: Dial Press, 2023.

Lorde, Audre. *Sister Outsider.* Berkeley, Calif.: Crossing Press, 1984.

Mallasz, Gitta. *Talking with Angels.* Einsiedeln, Switzerland: Daimon Verlag, 1988.

Pagels, Elaine. *Beyond Belief: The Secret Gospel of Thomas.* New York: Vintage Books, 2003.

Taussig, Hal, ed. *A New New Testament: A Bible for the Twenty-First Century Combining Traditional and Newly Discovered Texts.* Boston: Houghton Mifflin Harcourt, 2013.

Tesfamariam, Rahiel. *Imagine Freedom: Transforming Pain into Political and Spiritual Power.* New York: HarperCollins, 2024.

Vaid-Menon, Alok. *Beyond the Gender Binary.* New York: Penguin Workshop, 2020.

van der Kolk, Bessel. *The Body Keeps the Score: Brain, Mind, and Body in the Healing of Trauma.* New York: Penguin Books, 2014.

Vearncombe, Erin, Brandon Scott, and Hal Taussig. *After Jesus Before Christianity.* New York: HarperCollins, 2021.

von Franz, Marie-Louise. *Alchemy: An Introduction to the Symbolism and the Psychology.* Toronto: Inner City Books, 1980.

Watterson, Meggan. *The Divine Feminine Oracle: A 53-Card Deck & Guidebook for Embodying Love.* Carlsbad, Calif.: Hay House, 2018.

―――. *The Mary Magdalene Oracle: A 44-Card Deck & Guidebook of Mary's Gospel & Legend.* Carlsbad, Calif.: Hay House, 2023.

―――. *Mary Magdalene Revealed: The First Apostle, Her Feminist Gos-*

pel & the Christianity We Haven't Tried Yet. Carlsbad, Calif.: Hay House, 2019.

———. *Reveal: A Sacred Manual for Getting Spiritually Naked.* Carlsbad, Calif.: Hay House, 2013.

Weil, Simone. *Waiting for God.* New York: G. P. Putnam's Sons, 1951.

West, Cornel. *Race Matters.* Boston: Beacon Press Books, 1993.

Woodman, Marion. *Conscious Femininity.* Toronto: Inner City Books, 1993.

———. *The Pregnant Virgin: A Process of Psychological Transformation.* Toronto: Inner City Books, 1985.

NOTES

PREFACE: BAPTIZE

1. The word *god* is the masculine form of describing the divine. To capitalize the word *god* for me allows us to forget that there are other, more inclusive ways to describe the divine.

1. HER NAME

1. Simone Weil, *Waiting for God* (New York: G. P. Putnam's Sons, 1951), p. 9.
2. Erin Vearncombe, Brandon Scott, and Hal Taussig, *After Jesus Before Christianity* (New York: HarperCollins, 2021), pp. 3, 10.

2. WITHIN

1. Rainer Maria Rilke, *Letters to a Young Poet,* ed. and trans. Charlie Louth (New York: Penguin, 2014), p. 24.

3. ERASURE

1. Hal Taussig, ed., *A New New Testament: A Bible for the Twenty-First Century Combining Traditional and Newly Discovered Texts* (Boston: Houghton Mifflin Harcourt, 2013), p. 138 (Acts of the Apostles 9:4).
2. Ibid., p. 356 (1 Timothy 2:11–13).
3. Ibid., p. 299 (Galatians 3:27–28).

5. THE WORD

1. Taussig, ed., *A New New Testament,* p. 224.
2. Karen King, *The Gospel of Mary of Magdala: Jesus and the First Woman Apostle* (Santa Rosa, CA: Polebridge Press, 2003), p. 13.
3. Taussig, ed., *A New New Testament,* p. 46 (Matthew 18:6).
4. Ibid., p. 460 (Revelation 20:10).
5. James Brundage, *Law, Sex, and Christian Society in Medieval Europe* (Chicago: University of Chicago Press, 1987), p. 85.
6. Phillip Schaff, "*Tertullianus–De Cultu Feminarum* (On the Apparel of Women)," trans. Rev. S. Thelwall (Christian Classics Ethereal Library), p. 20, http://www.ccel.org/ccel/schaff/anf04.html.

7. Alok Vaid-Menon, *Beyond the Gender Binary* (New York: Penguin Workshop, 2020), p. 6.
8. Taussig, ed., *A New New Testament,* p. 517.
9. Ibid.

6. YES & NO & MAYBE

1. Taussig, ed., *A New New Testament,* pp. 183–85 (*The Thunder: Perfect Mind* 1:5–6, 9–10; 2:7–10; 4:32).
2. Vearncombe, Scott, and Taussig, *After Jesus Before Christianity,* p. 6.
3. King, *The Gospel of Mary of Magdala,* p. 15.
4. Jean-Yves Leloup, *The Gospel of Philip: Jesus, Mary Magdalene, and the Gnosis of Sacred Union* (Rochester, Vt.: Inner Traditions, 2003), p. 83.
5. Jean-Yves Leloup, *The Gospel of Mary Magdalene* (Rochester, Vt.: Inner Traditions, 2002), p. 11.
6. Mira Jacob, "Things I Thought Made Sense Just Don't Anymore," *New York Times,* December 28, 2023, http://nytimes.com/2023/12/28 /opinion/love-rage-evolution-pandemic.html.

7. VOICE

1. LeLoup, *The Gospel of Philip,* p. 57.
2. For example: Womanist Theology, Black Theology, Liberation Theology, Latina Theology, Abuelita Theology, Asian American Theology, Native American Theology, and Queer Theology.
3. Audre Lorde, *Sister Outsider* (Berkeley, Calif.: Crossing Press, 1984), p. 42.
4. Ibid., p. 41.
5. Ibid.
6. Sister Joan Chittister, *Heart of Flesh: Feminist Spirituality for Women and Men* (Grand Rapids, Mich.: Eerdmans, 1998), p. 116.

9. PURITY

1. Taussig, ed., *A New New Testament,* p. 30.
2. Ibid., p. 337.
3. Linda Kay Klein, "What Is Purity Culture?" https://lindakayklein.com /what-is-purity-culture/.
4. Taussig, ed., *A New New Testament,* p. 337.
5. Ibid., p. 225.
6. Ibid.
7. Ibid.
8. Ibid.
9. King, *The Gospel of Mary of Magdala,* p. 151.

10. WORTH

1. Taussig, ed., *A New New Testament,* p. 276 (1 Corinthians 13:12).

11. THE BODY'S BODY

1. Founded in 2006 by author and activist Tarana Burke.
2. See "*Sentencing Survivors: The Trials of Joan Little and Cyntoia Brown*," Planned Parenthood Advocates of Arizona, August 5, 2019, http://planned parenthoodaction.org/planned-parenthood-advocates-arizona/blog /sentencing-survivors-the-trials-of-joan-little-and-cyntoia-brown.

12. COURAGE

1. Chinua Achebe, interview with Jerome Brooks, "The Art of Fiction No. 139," *The Paris Review* 133 (Winter 1994), https://www.theparisreview .org/interviews/1720/the-art-of-fiction-no-139-chinua-achebe.
2. See Maura Turcotte, "Gold Medalist Aly Raisman Is Suing Olympic Organization for Failing to Stop Larry Nassar," *Ms.*, March 5, 2018, https:// msmagazine.com/2018/03/05/gold-medalist-aly-raisman-suing-olympic -organizations-failing-stop-larry-nassar.
3. Malala Yousafzai, Nobel Lecture, December 10, 2014, https://www .nobelprize.org/uploads/2018/06/yousafzai-lecture_en.pdf.

13. PURPOSE

1. King, *The Gospel of Mary of Magdala,* p. 14.
2. Ibid., p. 15.
3. Ibid.
4. Brené Brown, "Pressing on with Purpose," August 31, 2020, https://brene brown.com/articles/2020/08/31/pressing-on-with-purpose/.

14. POSSESSION

1. Taussig, ed., *A New New Testament,* p. 339.
2. Ibid.
3. John Cassian, *The Institutes,* trans. Boniface Ramsey (Mahwah, N.J.: Newman Press of Paulist Press, 2000).
4. Taussig, ed., *A New New Testament,* p. 339.

15. LOVE

1. "Listening Again to Loving," Children's Defense Fund, https://www .childrensdefense.org/listening-again-to-loving.
2. "Same-Sex Marriage Legalization Linked to Reduction in Suicide Attempts Among High School Students," Johns Hopkins Bloomberg School of Public Health, February 20, 2017, https://publichealth.jhu.edu/2017/same -sex-marriage-legalization-linked-to-reduction-in-suicide-attempts-among -high-school-students.
3. See United Nations, Human Rights, Office of the High Commissioner, Child and Forced Marriage, including in Humanitarian Settings, https:// www.ohchr.org/en/women/child-and-forced-marriage-including -humanitarian-settings, accessed April 24, 2025.

4. See Sarah House, Shannon Seery, Nicole Cervi, and Jeremiah Kohl, "Party of One: How Single Women Stack Up in the U.S. Economy," Wells Fargo Economics, March 8, 2023, https://externalcontent.blob.core.windows.net/pdfs /7a16f5a8-b531-403c-bb1e-ed14d5cbd8b2.pdf. This report found a record-breaking 52 percent of women in the United States as of 2021 are unmarried.
5. Taussig, ed., *A New New Testament*, p. 339.
6. Ibid.
7. Margaret Atwood, *Selected Poems II: 1976–1986* (Boston: Houghton Mifflin Harcourt, 2012), p. 115.

16. NAKEDNESS

1. Taussig, ed., *A New New Testament*, p. 338.
2. Ibid., p. 339.
3. Ibid., p. 276 (1 Corinthians 13:12).
4. Ibid., p. 339.
5. King, *The Gospel of Mary of Magdala*, p. 16.
6. Cynthia Bourgeault, *The Meaning of Mary Magdalene: Discovering the Woman at the Heart of Christianity* (Boulder, Colo.: Shambala Press, 2010), p. 103.
7. Taussig, ed., *A New New Testament*, p. 339.

17. DEATH

1. Taussig, ed., *A New New Testament*, p. 299.
2. Ibid., p. 300.
3. Ibid., p. 276. "*Meanwhile, faith, hope, and love endure—these three, but the greatest of these is love*" (1 Corinthians 13:13).
4. "Black Female Voices: Who Is Listening? A Public Dialogue Between bell hooks and Melissa Harris-Perry," The New School, New York, N.Y., December 16, 2013, YouTube, https://www.youtube.com/watch?v= 5OmgqXao1ng.
5. Taussig, ed., *A New New Testament*, p. 340.
6. Ibid.
7. Ibid.
8. Ibid.
9. Ibid.
10. King, *The Gospel of Mary of Magdala*, p. 16.
11. Meggan Watterson, *The Mary Magdalene Oracle: A 44-Card Deck & Guidebook of Mary's Gospel & Legend* (Carlsbad, Calif.: Hay House, 2023).

18. PRAYER

1. Taussig, ed., *A New New Testament*, p. 225.
2. *Writings from the Philokalia on Prayer of the Heart*, trans. E. Kadloubovsky and G.E.H. Palmer (New York: Faber & Faber, 1979), p. 30.
3. Thomas Merton, *Confessions of a Guilty Bystander* (New York: Image, 2014), p. 192.

4. Taussig, ed., *A New New Testament*, p. 225.
5. Jeffrey J. Kripal, *The Superhumanities: Historical Precedents, Moral Objections, New Realities* (Chicago: University of Chicago Press, 2022), p. 9.
6. Taussig, ed., *A New New Testament*, p. 211 (John 17:17).
7. Ibid., p. 340.
8. Ibid.
9. Ibid.
10. Ibid.
11. Ibid.
12. Ibid., p. 341.
13. Ibid.
14. Ibid.
15. Ibid.

19. SACRED RAGE

1. Taussig, ed., *A New New Testament*, p. 341.
2. Ibid.
3. Ibid.
4. Ibid., p. 183.
5. Ibid., p. 341.
6. Ibid.
7. Ibid., p. 185.
8. Ibid., p. 341.
9. Ibid., p. 224.

20. SACRILEGE

1. Taussig, ed., *A New New Testament*, p. 341.
2. Ibid.
3. Ibid.
4. Ibid.
5. Ibid.
6. Ibid.
7. Ibid.
8. Vearncombe, Scott, and Taussig, *After Jesus Before Christianity*, p. 122.
9. Ibid., p. 120.

21. AUTHORITY

1. Taussig, ed., *A New New Testament*, p. 342.
2. Ibid.
3. Ibid.
4. Ibid.
5. Ibid.
6. Ibid., p. 224.

22. FREEDOM

1. Taussig, ed., *A New New Testament*, p. 342.
2. Ibid.
3. Ibid.
4. Ibid., p. 343.
5. Ibid.
6. Vearncombe, Scott, and Taussig, *After Jesus Before Christianity*, p. 28.
7. Ibid., p. 37.
8. Ibid., p. 11.
9. Ibid., p. 6.
10. Ibid., p. 7.
11. Ibid., p. 45.
12. Ibid., p. 166.

23. THE WOMEN ALL CRIED OUT IN A LOUD VOICE

1. Taussig, ed., *A New New Testament*, p. 343.
2. Ibid.
3. King, *The Gospel of Mary of Magdala*, p. 17.
4. Taussig, ed., *A New New Testament*, p. 226.
5. King, *The Gospel of Mary of Magdala*, p. 17.
6. Taussig, ed., *A New New Testament*, p. 226.
7. Vearncombe, Scott, and Taussig, *After Jesus Before Christianity*, p. 45.
8. Taussig, ed., *A New New Testament*, p. 343.
9. Ibid.
10. Ibid.

24. THE GIRL WHO BAPTIZED HERSELF

1. Taussig, ed., *A New New Testament*, p. 343.
2. Ibid.
3. Ibid.
4. Ibid.
5. Vearncombe, Scott, and Taussig, *After Jesus Before Christianity*, p. 213.
6. Taussig, ed., *A New New Testament*, p. 343.
7. Vearncombe, Scott, and Taussig, *After Jesus Before Christianity*, p. 213.
8. Ibid., 323.

25. THE HOT GOSPEL

1. Taussig, ed., *A New New Testament*, p. 344.
2. Ibid.
3. King, *The Gospel of Mary of Magdala*, p. 15.
4. Taussig, ed., *A New New Testament*, p. 344.
5. Ibid.
6. King, *The Gospel of Mary of Magdala*, p. 189.
7. Taussig, ed., *A New New Testament*, p. 344.

8. Gitta Mallasz, *Talking with Angels* (Einsiedeln, Switzerland: Daimon Verlag, 1988), pp. 141–42.

9. Quoted in Jeffrey J. Kripal, *Roads of Excess, Palaces of Wisdom: Eroticism & Reflexivity in the Study of Mysticism* (Chicago: Chicago University Press, 2001), p. 33.

10. bell hooks, *All About Love* (New York: William Morrow, 2000), p. 247.

11. Thomas Merton, excerpt from "Two Songs for M.," *Eighteen Poems* (New York: New Directions Publishing, 1968).

CONCLUSION: A VERY FEW PEOPLE

1. Interview with James Baldwin in the film *Meeting the Man: James Baldwin in Paris,* directed by Terence Dixon, 1971.

2. Marion Woodman, *The Pregnant Virgin: A Process of Psychological Transformation* (Toronto: Inner City Books, 1985), p. 117.

ABOUT THE AUTHOR

MEGGAN WATTERSON is the *Wall Street Journal* bestselling author of *Mary Magdalene Revealed, The Mary Magdalene Oracle, The Divine Feminine Oracle,* and *REVEAL*. She is a feminist theologian with a Master of Theological Studies from Harvard Divinity and a Master of Divinity from Union Theological Seminary at Columbia University. She created The House of Mary Magdalene—a spiritual community that studies texts left out of the traditional canon, and practices the soul-voice meditation. Her work has appeared in, among other outlets, *The New York Times, HuffPost,* TEDxWomen, and *Marie Claire*.

www.megganwatterson.com

ABOUT THE TYPE

This book was set in Galliard, a typeface designed in 1978 by Matthew Carter (b. 1937) for the Mergenthaler Linotype Company. Galliard is based on the sixteenth-century typefaces of Robert Granjon (1513–89).